CAMBRIDGE IBERIAN AND LATIN AMERICAN STUDIES

GENERAL EDITOR

P. E. RUSSELL, F.B.A.

EMERITUS PROFESSOR OF SPANISH STUDIES

UNIVERSITY OF OXFORD

The Spanish picaresque novel and the point of view

The Spanish picaresque novel and the point of view

FRANCISCO RICO

TRANSLATED BY CHARLES DAVIS
WITH HARRY SIEBER

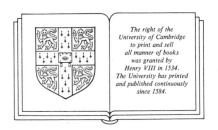

The right of the
University of Cambridge
to print and sell
all manner of books
was granted by
Henry VIII in 1534.
The University has printed
and published continuously
since 1584.

CAMBRIDGE UNIVERSITY PRESS

CAMBRIDGE

LONDON   NEW YORK   NEW ROCHELLE

MELBOURNE   SYDNEY

Published by the Press Syndicate of the University of Cambridge
The Pitt Building, Trumpington Street, Cambridge CB2 1RP
32 East 57th Street, New York, NY 10022, USA
296 Beaconsfield Parade, Middle Park, Melbourne 3206, Australia

© Francisco Rico 1969
© in English translation Cambridge University Press 1984

First published 1984

Printed in Great Britain
at the University Press, Cambridge

Library of Congress catalogue card number: 83-15040

British Library cataloguing in publication data
Rico, Francisco
The Spanish picaresque novel and the point of
view. – (Cambridge Iberian and Latin American studies)
1. Picaresque literature – History and criticism
2. Spanish fiction – Classical period, 1500–1700
– History and criticism
1. Title   11. Davis, Charles   111. La
novela picaresca y el punto de vista. *English*
863'.5   PQ6147.P5
ISBN 0 521 25370 5 hard covers
ISBN 0 521 27824 4 paperback

CE

AHORA,
PARA GUILLERMO Y FÉLIX

Contents

Author's preface

This little book was born in the form of a course of three lectures given at the Johns Hopkins University in the autumn of 1966, and subsequently presented with some variations – and sometimes abridged – in other places in Spain and the United States. The text published in 1970, despite the addition of a few paragraphs and the inclusion of a perhaps excessive number of notes, did not aspire to take my treatment of the subject beyond what was to be expected of three fairly lightweight talks. In the second edition (1972 and reprints) I reworked a couple of pages, where an inaccuracy had crept in; and in the third (1982) I replaced a passage in chapter 1 by another which, I hope, is more valid and precise, while at the same time introducing a dozen shorter emendations and modifications.

The present translation, naturally, follows the text of the third edition. However, it omits the original preface, which makes sense only if it is read in relation to Spanish novel-writing of the late sixties (indeed, these essays did not fail to exert a modest influence on fiction in Spanish in the following decade); and, in return, it adds a postscript which underlines some of the premises and limits of these pages. Of course, since 1970 there has been no shortage of critical contributions which enable one to develop, in one direction or another, the ideas set out here, but I do not believe that they affect my arguments and conclusions in any substantial respect. As well as the postscript, I have therefore included quite a number of references to recent publications, and occasionally expressed some opinion about them. But this material, like that extracted from subsequent works of my own, has always been put in a note and enclosed in square brackets, in order to avoid any confusion: humble though it may be, this book does have a place in the development of picaresque studies, and it would make no sense to try to revise the text *a ritroso*, in such a way as to commit the fraud of presenting as known and assumed certain themes and problems which did not enter into its original design. It should be noted, in addition, that now as in 1970 the bibliography cited is merely an indication and never aims to provide even moderately complete documentation.

It remains only for me to thank Sarah Stanton, of Cambridge University Press, who has taken so much interest in this translation; and my friend and colleague Harry Sieber for his help and collaboration. And, of course, my friend Charles Davis, tireless in his efforts to tame a rebellious style and temper the reluctance of the original Spanish to submit to the terminology of any school of criticism: just consider the fact that *trama* covers all the areas which in the English tradition might possibly be distinguished as 'story', 'plot', 'action', 'pattern' ..., and that these essays were written with the fluidity of the word *trama* in normal Spanish very much in mind, in accordance with a very conscious intention of avoiding or reducing to a minimum, here, the technical vocabulary of 'the critical idiom'.

Translator's preface

Although *Vuestra Merced*, in the *Lazarillo*, is commonly rendered 'Your Grace', I consider this to be too specific and elevated in its social connotations, and have chosen instead the more general title 'Your Worship' (used, moreover, by David Rowland in the first English translation). For *el caso*, a key term in chapter 1, 'the case' seems inescapable, and has been used throughout; among other things, the legal implications must be retained. Translations of quotations from original texts are my own. I have reproduced Professor Rico's page references, but for the *Guzmán* and the *Buscón* I have provided additional references to assist those using translations or other editions. The numbers in question indicate the part, book and chapter respectively, in the case of the *Guzmán* (there are three books in each part and between eight and ten chapters in each book); for the *Buscón*, they indicate book and chapter.

I

Lazarillo de Tormes, or polysemy

The first thing is the eye that sees; the second, the object seen; the third, the distance between them.

Albrecht Dürer

... three factors are involved: the thing which is to be known, the being who knows, and knowledge itself; let us examine them one by one and we shall discover that nothing is known.

Francisco Sánchez, *Quod nihil scitur*

His Worship receives a letter

The situation is well known: the novel, a late fruit of European letters, doesn't quite dare show its face; it appears and disappears, coyly suggesting first that it's here and then that it isn't, disguised as history or hidden behind the mask of a literary genre accepted by everyone. In the years around 1550, a writer of chivalric romances (the sort that people like the innkeeper Palomeque, Maritornes and the occasional gentleman from La Mancha considered so convincing) had no real qualms about presenting the far from ordinary adventures of his heroes as a rigorously truthful *crónica particular* ('private chronicle'). Meanwhile humanists and other readers who were familiar with the *studia humaniora* enjoyed the recently discovered *Ethiopian History* and did not hesitate to put Heliodorus's work on a par with the prestigious epics of classical antiquity.

But now something happens. Around 1554 – Charles V is thinking about retiring to the monastery of Yuste – the presses bring out a devilishly unique little book: *La vida de Lazarillo de Tormes, y de sus fortunas y adversidades* (The Life of Lazarillo de Tormes: his Fortunes and Misfortunes). A remarkable life indeed. Lázaro de Tormes is not the 'son of King Perion of Gaul and Queen Helisene', as was Amadis, but rather of the miller Tomé González and the laundress Antona Pérez. Nor does he come to marry an Ethiopian princess and see himself crowned as a great priest, like Theagenes. 'The height of all good fortune', for Lázaro, is marriage to a cleric's concubine and an appointment as town crier. And between the beginning of the tale and the denouement there are no great feats, brilliant settings or lofty exemplary deeds: Lázaro has served a blind beggar, a village priest, a poor squire and people of that ilk; he has rubbed shoulders with stable boys, tripe-vendors and water-carriers; he has frequented hostelries and picked up a lot of mud along the roads; ... he has not much more to talk about.

What sort of author would have dared to serve up such a string of trivia as a private chronicle, at a time when Luis Vives even considered it trivial for an historian to mention the price of wheat during a drought?[1] Besides, what literary genre hallowed by the precepts of the critics could serve as camouflage for so curious a specimen? Literary convention was not yet on very good terms with the low-born[2] (this book evidently seemed so out of the ordinary that Lázaro had to set himself up as a sociologist and assert that little or no credit was due to those who 'inherited noble estates'). Narrative prose in particular had no close precedents to offer in which such continuous and exclusive attention was devoted to a character of so lowly a station as Lázaro González Pérez.[3] What was one to do then? It is pointless to speculate about other possible solutions, but it is important to recognize properly the solution found by the anonymous author of the *Lazarillo*. There had in fact always existed a literary model that had managed splendidly to reconcile rhetorical tradition with that modest degree of historicity which seemed to be a necessary basis for the early stirrings of the form we would learn to call the novel: the epistle.

The Life of Lazarillo de Tormes is, in fact, to a large extent simply a letter.[4] The Prologue concludes precisely by pointing out that fact: 'Your Worship *writes that I should write to you* and tell you about the case very fully' (p. 62);[5] and the first words of the narrative itself, introduced by an illative *pues* ('well then'), clearly show that Lázaro sees what he is doing as meeting an epistolary obligation: 'Well then, Your Worship should know, first of all, that they call me Lázaro de Tormes ...' ('Pues sepa Vuestra Merced, ante todas cosas, que a mí llaman Lázaro de Tormes...', p. 63). His Worship (we too shall use this title to refer to that mysterious figure) has evidently addressed himself to Lázaro by letter to ask for information about an as yet unspecified matter.

And Lázaro has answered, also by letter, a fact emphasized by a phrase which was an almost automatic commonplace in such circumstances: 'you write that I should write to you'.[6] Lázaro never forgets whom he is addressing, nor what the conventions of the genre demand: the epistle is one side of a conversation ('velut pars altera dialogi'),[7] and our narrative will be interspersed with appeals to its addressee ('I am glad to tell Your Worship...', p. 67; 'so that Your Worship may see...', p. 74, etc.). And since ancient custom as opposed to modern prescribed that the writer should leave the declaration of the place and date of a letter until the end,[8] the work closes on a chronological note – 'this has been happening in the same year...' ('esto fue el mesmo año') – and with an explicit reference to 'this illustrious city of Toledo' (p. 145).

The received approach insists on characterizing the Renaissance as an age that concentrated on the individual. Rarely is this feature of the period sufficiently rigorously analysed, and I shall not do so either; such a view does not, however, seem any the less correct for that. The Renaissance is certainly the period of free interpretation of the Bible and of personal religion, of the personalization of social and economic relationships – which had been very much more closely linked, in the Middle Ages, to the family and the group – the period of the portrait, and of the first civil registries.[9] Paul Oskar Kristeller, a scholar rarely given to brilliant but badly documented generalizations, has managed to distinguish the flowering of individualism as one of the factors behind the unparalleled success of epistolary literature between the fourteenth and sixteenth centuries.[10] The letter has always lent itself to confidences and confessions; moreover, by 1554 it was well established as a vehicle for autobiography. Angelo Poliziano[11] singled out two kinds of letters: the first, 'gravis et severa'; the second, 'otiosa', seasoned with jokes and with a goodly number of proverbs, and in a somewhat more sophisticated style than the dialogue. Now both these types of epistle were thoroughly inured to the subject matter of autobiography.[12] From Plato (no less) to Petrarch, Lapo da Castiglionchio or Francisco López de Villalobos, the *gravis et severa* type of autobiographical missive was often written to justify a particular attitude or situation – at someone else's request, genuinely or ostensibly – by viewing it in the perspective of a whole life (and in more than one case by insisting on interpreting it as a triumph of virtue, more meritorious than anything that could be obtained through hereditary nobility). The *otiosa* subgenre, characteristically diverting and festive, was so well known that it even had its own category and designation (*iocosa da se, lettera faceta*) both in the manuals of letter-writing demanded by humanist pedagogy and in the compilations of *carte messagiere* which had a spectacular success starting with a volume published by Pietro Aretino in 1537. The *iocosa, faceta* or (in Spain) *graciosa* type tended to centre on a single episode or anecdote in which the object of mockery or humour was the author of the letter himself; it delighted in gossip, spicy (or even obscene) allusions, ironic treatment of day-to-day trifles; and it could easily become apocryphal or be attributed to totally fictitious characters: the most humble slaves of the *Serenissima* Republic of Venice, in Andrea Calmo (1547, 1548, 1552); the *valurose donne* defending their reputation against calumny, in Ortesio Lando (1548); or, in the vein of soliloquy, the ridiculous *mal maritato* of Cesare Rao (1562).

It is on to that tradition, then, that the *Lazarillo* is grafted. Do not misunderstand me: this does not mean that our particular story deliberately sets out either to parody the tradition or to extend it; what happens is rather that the *Lazarillo* bases itself on that tradition in order to make itself identifiable as a literary entity. Nor do I claim that an epistolary lineage of this kind was the only stimulus that suggested to the mysterious author the idea of effecting the transfer from real life to artistic representation by writing a novel in the form of an autobiography.[13] It is very probable that he was also inspired by Apuleius and that the adventures of the Golden Ass, narrated in the fictional character's own words, led our author to use the first person.[14] But if that was the case, the source of the inspiration remained outside the novel (although this does not mean that it was any less important an influence in another sense). As an autobiographical letter, by contrast, the book not only satisfied the discrete demand for an appearance of historicity which was a normal condition of fiction at that time, on the one hand, but also reinforced it by a decisive injection of realism, of verisimilitude, on the other. After all, Lázaro, logically enough, relates what only he can know:[15] moreover what Lázaro narrates, as we shall see shortly, is to a great extent also the reason why he recounts anything at all – to put it in another conundrum, Lázaro's letter seeks to explain why he has been asked to write a letter. In this way the literary genre to which the *Lazarillo* supposedly belongs forms part of the argument itself.[16]

The case

Obviously the epistolary framework could not simply be adopted without further justification in a tale 'which claimed to relate something that actually happened ..., presented as something real'.[17] For who would have found it credible that such a nonentity should have bothered to write up his 'fortunes and misfortunes'? A pretext was needed. And, of course, there was one. Let us return to the final part of the Prologue: 'And since Your Worship writes that I should write to you and tell you about *the case* very fully, I thought it best to begin it not in the middle but from the beginning, so as to give you a complete account of myself' ('Y pues Vuestra Merced escribe se le escriba y relate *el caso* muy por extenso, parecióme no tomalle por el medio, sino del principio, porque se tenga entera noticia de mi persona', p. 62). The question arises: what is this 'case' that has awakened His Worship's curiosity and thereby led Lázaro de Tormes, lowly town crier of Toledo, to take up his pen and write so 'very fully' that, in his desire to clarify it thoroughly, explaining it from the very beginning, he has ended up sketching an autobiography? In order to find the answer, one must first point out that not only does Lázaro make copious remarks addressed to the person who requested his report ('I am glad to tell Your Worship', etc.), but that in the last chapter, His Worship even makes an appearance in the narrative. By then, in fact, the protagonist holds an office under the crown, 'in which', he says, 'I now live and reside in God's and Your Worship's service', and declares himself to be happy under the protection of the 'Archpriest of San Salvador, my master, and Your Worship's servant and friend' (pp. 141–2); all this at the same time as the city is entertaining Charles V with 'great celebrations and festivities, as Your Worship has no doubt heard' (p. 145).[18] Now even if we had no other evidence on which to base an opinion, the very consistency of the novel would seem logically to demand that, if His Worship had asked him to write about 'the case', this must have occurred during the period in Lázaro's life when the *pícaro* and his master came to know each other;[19] that is, the period recorded in the final chapter.

How could one forget those pages? Lázaro has settled and found a secure position in Toledo. Through his own efforts and the favour of others he has got a job as town crier; and this post has given him access to certain useful friendships. One has been especially productive: that of a certain cleric, the Archpriest of San Salvador, who has given Lázaro the job of hawking the wine he has for sale, and, seeing the lad's good qualities, he offered to marry him to a servant girl of his. Lázaro accepted and has had no reason not to congratulate himself. The good Archpriest has turned out to be a great protector of the little couple: he has rented a house for them next to his own, showers them with gifts, invites them to eat with him... It is certainly true that there has been no shortage of malicious gossips 'saying I don't know what and I do know what' ('diciendo no sé qué y sí sé qué', p. 143): about the fact that Lázaro's wife comes and goes in the Archpriest's house (naturally, she goes to 'make his bed and cook his food'); about the fact that before they were married she 'had had three abortions...' ('había parido tres veces...'). Lázaro does not intend to allow such slander to upset the peace and prosperity he enjoys: he is willing to swear 'on the Holy Sacrament' that his wife 'is as good a woman as any living within the gates of Toledo' (p. 145).

'The case' is simply this: the gossip that has spread around the city about the dubious trio, the suspicion of a *ménage à trois* which is complacently accepted by Lázaro. But Lázaro, as we already know, scorns the slanderous rumours and does not even conde-scend to discuss them. Only because His Worship is the person he is and has written that Lázaro 'should write to him and tell him about *the case* very fully' has our town crier agreed to air the subject, vindicating his wife's unspotted honour. Now that the situation has been satisfactorily cleared up he can add a final touch and announce that he has fulfilled his responsibility: 'Up till now nobody has ever heard us say anything about *the case*' ('Hasta el día de hoy nunca nadie nos oyó sobre *el caso*', p. 144).

'The case' is, then, the pretext for the writing of *The Life of Lazarillo de Tormes*. But not only that: it is also the ultimate subject of the novel. It is important not to lose sight of the vital point made in the Prologue: if we have a 'complete account' of the protagonist, we owe it to the fact that Lázaro has decided not to begin to relate the case 'in the middle, but from the beginning'. Thus the autobiography depends on 'the case' and at the same time justifies it; or (to apply the familiar terminology of Ferdinand de Saussure), it presents itself as the 'diachronic' dimension of 'the case', that is, as its trajectory along one of the several 'axes of successions' that constitute Lázaro's total existence. Lázaro, the person, accepts his past in terms of his present[20] as a town crier, satisfied with 'the thousand blessings' that God is sending him through his wife and the Archpriest; and the *Lazarillo*, the letter, is organized out of the various earlier episodes as they converge towards 'the case' of the final chapter.

The blind man and His Worship

The nucleus of the *Lazarillo*, then, lies in its conclusion: 'the case', coming at the very end and constituting the reason for the work's composition, is the point around which the other elements – that prefigure and illustrate it – have gradually accumulated, finally making up the novel as a whole. Of course, not every scrap of information about Lázaro's background can be read in direct relation to his shabby present as a sham husband: but certainly all the narrative cells that define the total structure, all the threads that determine the design of the tapestry, are subordinated to it.

Lázaro's adventures with the blind man, for example, are ostensibly organized around five basic motifs: (1) Lázaro's 'great blow on the head' (*calabazada*) against the stone bull; (2) the subtle schemes he contrives in order to drink his master's wine, subsequently paying the price when he is bashed with the jug; (3) the trick with the grapes; (4) the theft of the sausage and the consequent beating; and (5) the blind man's smashing against a stone post. It seems clear, moreover, that (1) and (5) are the opposite sides of the same coin (Lázaro demonstrates that he has learned his lesson, by taking revenge on the beggar with a parallel stratagem),[21] and that (2) and (4) follow the same pattern and reinforce one another. But both pairs acquire relevance in the structure of the novel in so far as they are related to 'the case' at the end.

The substance of (1) and (5) is well known. The blind man assures the lad that, if he places his ear near the bull which is at the entrance to the Roman bridge in Salamanca, he will hear 'a great noise inside it'; Lázaro does so and for his naïveté he gets a good hard blow on the head together with a sarcastic comment: 'You young fool, that'll teach you that a blind man's boy must know one trick more than the devil himself' (p. 67). It is the boy's true birth certificate: 'It seemed to me that in that instant I awoke out of the naïveté in which, as a child, I was asleep. I said to myself: "This man is telling the truth; I ought to be on the lookout and alert, for I'm alone, and I should think about how to fend for myself."' No one has failed to see the overwhelming importance of the scene: the blow on the head forces Lazarillo to become aware of his solitude and to face up to a hostile world; it provides us with the first key to his attitude toward life. But assuming that is so, the important thing to notice here is the remark which the narrator adds after this episodic nucleus: 'I am glad to tell Your Worship about these childish trifles so as to show how commendable it is for lowly people to manage to rise in the world' (pp. 67–8). Lázaro, as we have already pointed out, has risen to 'the height of all good fortune' (p. 145), thanks to his wife and the Archpriest, 'Your Worship's servant and friend' (p. 142). And calling attention to His Worship shows precisely the connection between 'the case' and the episode of the bull: the town crier of Toledo faithfully fulfils His Worship's wishes by emphasizing those points in his journey through life that throw most light on the critical circumstance, 'the case', about which he has been asked for information.

In this way many of the appeals to the half-concealed addressee have a threefold structural function: on the one hand they reveal explicitly the epistolary character of the narrative; on the other, they clearly succeed in projecting fragments of his past life on to the protagonist of 'the case'; and in both these ways they reinforce the illusion of historicity and the verisimilitude of the novel as a whole.

The pattern emerges still more clearly in (2) and (4). The blind man detects Lázaro stealing wine right under his nose and punishes him by bashing him on the head with the jug.[22] Of course, he takes pity afterwards, and washes the wound with the very object of the crime, adding with a smile: 'What do you think of this, Lázaro? What made you sick heals you and makes you well' (p. 73). Later, when the boy steals a sausage from him and is soundly beaten in return, the beggar cleans the bruises with the same crude antiseptic, commenting as he does so:

'Truly, this lad costs me more wine washing him in one year than I drink in two. At least, Lázaro, you owe more to wine than to your own father, because he bred you once, but wine has given you life a thousand times over.' And then he recounted how many times he had smashed my head and scratched my face and then healed them with wine. 'I tell you', he said, 'that if any man is to be lucky with wine, it will be you.' (p. 79)

These two vignettes not only reinforce the link between (1) and (5), echoing the blows received by the poor boy and motivating the retaliatory blow: they also are unified by their emphasis of the wine motif (the wine that Lázaro drinks, the wine he goes to fetch when he substitutes the turnip for the sausage, the wine which heals him so many times), culminating in the second scene. Why in fact was Lázaro going to be 'lucky with wine'? Because 'the case' began with wine: not for nothing does the town crier say that 'the Archpriest of San Salvador, my master, and Your Worship's friend and servant, arranged to have me marry a servant girl of his *because I was hawking his wines*' (p.142). In this way the blind man's prophecy connects the incidents of Lázaro's childhood to 'the case', which, in principle, is the only thing that interests His Worship. This is precisely why the narrator is so quick to tell him that he has had to dwell on these incidents 'considering that what [the blind man] told me that day proved to be as true *as Your Worship will hear later on*' (p. 79).

The exception proves the rule. Nothing in (3) seems to have a clearly-defined structural purpose. Master and servant agree to devour a bunch of grapes, each taking one at a time; naturally, both break the agreement; and when the grapes are finished, 'shaking his head', the blind man hazards a guess: 'Lázaro, you have deceived me. I'd swear to God that you've been eating three grapes at a time... Do you know how I can see you've been eating three at a time? It is because I was eating two at a time and you said nothing' (p. 75). Very clever, certainly. But why tell this story rather than any other of 'the evil tricks that the blind man played'? The narrator explains his choice: 'so that Your Worship may see how shrewd this blind man was I'll tell you *one case among many* that happened to me while I was with him, in which I think he showed clearly how very clever he was' ('porque vea Vuestra Merced a cuánto se estendía el ingenio de este astuto ciego, contaré *un caso de muchos* que con él me acaescieron, en el cual me parece dio bien a entender su gran astucia', p. 74); and, having finished giving his example, he comments: 'so as not to be long-winded, *I am leaving out many things* which are both funny and noteworthy and which happened to me in the service of this my first master' (p. 75). For Lázaro's purposes of illustration, one example is enough; and of course, since it concerns the master more than the servant, since it is not, strictly speaking, a functional element in the novelistic structure (it does nothing to advance the plot), it is offered to His Worship accompanied by explanations and provisos. For the person who asked Lázaro to write about 'the case' could otherwise have complained: 'What has all this got to do with me?'.

Towards the poetics of the Lazarillo

In the novel, Lázaro's past is filtered through his present. 'Well then, Your Worship should know first of all that they call me Lázaro de Tormes...'. In the first line of the story the town crier quite rightly says 'they call me', because, as we discover later, it is only at the very end, in the concrete present in which he is writing, that people actually 'call' him by his full name. And he does not fail to emphasize it, proudly, by using the third person, even though he could have continued with the usual *I* form: 'if anyone, throughout the whole city, has wine to sell, or anything else, and

Lázaro de Tormes is not involved in it, they can be sure they will not do well' (p. 142).

By this process and others, the framework is established from the very outset. The parallel between the first and final pages sharply defines a literary space. Tomé González steals grain from the sacks that are taken to the mill and suffers 'persecución por justicia' ('persecution for righteousness's sake', p. 63); his son, the town crier, loudly broadcasts the crimes of those who 'padecen persecuciones por justicia' ('are punished by the authorities', p. 142)* and manages to get given 'about five bushels of grain' (p. 143). Antona Pérez, finding herself destitute, 'decided to associate with good people', 'rented a little house' in the city, 'started to cook for some students and washed clothes for some stable lads' (p. 64), only to end up living in sin with the negro Zaide; Lázaro marries a concubine, who is kept busy 'making the bed and cooking' (p. 143) for the Archpriest; he gets them to rent 'a little house' ('una casilla') for him in Toledo, and then explains: 'I decided to associate with good people' (p. 144). Zaide provides for Antona and her boys with the proceeds of his pilfering; the Archpriest regales Lázaro and his wife with the ill-gotten gains he has acquired by abusing his priesthood – the narrator leaves this in no doubt when after narrating Zaide's thefts he adds a comment which becomes fully comprehensible only in the light of 'the case':[23] 'We should not be surprised when *a priest* or friar steals, one of them from the poor and the other from the convent for his female devotees ..., considering love induced a poor slave to do this' (p. 65). Or for one last example, when fate decreed that Zaide's theft and Antona's concubinage should arouse suspicion, Lázaro, 'like a child', denounced the guilty couple, revealing 'everything he knew', which gave rise to 'a thousand troubles'. But when gossiping tongues begin to wag about 'the case', which provides him with 'a thousand blessings', the town crier keeps

* [*Translator's note.* There is an untranslatable joke here based on the ambiguity of *por justicia*, which means both 'for the sake of righteousness' (a parodic allusion to the *propter iustitiam* of Matthew 5.10), and 'by the (judicial) authorities'. The translations adopted in the text indicate the ostensible primary meaning in the two passages where the phrase is used, but in each case the other meaning is also implied. See Stephen Gilman, 'Matthew, v: 10, in Castilian jest and earnest', in *Studia hispanica in honorem R. Lapesa*, vol. I (Madrid, 1972), pp. 257–65.]

mum: and what he writes to His Worship, out of respectful deference, is the very opposite of a confession of guilt.

'In order to turn an object into an artistic fact', wrote Victor Shklovski, 'one must extract it from the succession of facts of which life is composed.'[24] Good literature, at least, often seeks to construct linguistic objects which are particularly well delineated and, by the same token, presented as the object of a heightened form of perception: fully integrated, complete objects, which lay claim to autonomy. Repetition, parallelism and contrast are among the most universal devices used to define the outlines and strengthen the complete (and unique) character of a literary work. For example, repetition of the phonic figure of the line, in poetry, immediately delimits the poem; rhyme forces the reader to recall earlier elements, relates them to each other and, in so doing, continually revitalizes the context, reinforcing the coherence of the message. Symmetries and contrasts in a novel can perform a similar function: they can define the limits of the subject, mark out an area, of which each section forces us to keep the others in mind, and lastly bring out the motivation of the plot – and thus suggest a spurious underlying coherence in life. This is undoubtedly what happens in the *Lazarillo*: the analogies between the first and last chapters delimit that material from the protagonist's life which constitutes the subject of the novel, and thereby throw into relief the ways in which all its elements are connected.

Another way to delineate the literary object, emphasizing its integrity and independence, involves creating a continuous expectation and satisfying it with unexpected directness, so that the final point, the end of the trajectory, is felt with greater force. In the sonnet we find this process used to perfection. One of Petrarch's (CCXXIV),[25] among so many others, contains a progress-ive protasis of thirteen conditional lines:

> S'una fede amorosa, un cor non finto,
> un languir dolce, un desiar cortese;
> s'oneste voglie in gentil foco accese,
> un lungo error in cieco laberinto ...
> son le cagion ch'amando i'mi distempre ...,
>
> If a loving devotion, a sincere heart
> A sweet pining, a virtuous desire;

If honourable longings aflame in noble fire,
A long wandering in a blind labyrinth ...
Are the reason why in loving I destroy myself ...

and brings out their full meaning only in the apodosis of the final line:

vostro, donna, 'l peccato, e mio fia 'l danno.

Yours, lady, is the fault, and mine the injury.

Here, each line adds new tension to the tension of the preceding line; and when this tension is broken in the final nucleus, which draws together the substance of all that has gone before it, the sonnet finally emerges as a perfectly resolved whole with no possible continuation. A poem based on correlation (of the type rediscovered by Dámaso Alonso)[26] often closes in on itself, gathering up in the conclusion all the previously disseminated elements (there is nothing like a final roll call for making sure that the whole company has taken part). In one very famous poem, the suspension created by the successive uses of the anaphoric *while* ('mientras') is resolved by gathering together the dispersed parts and juxtaposing them with another, strictly parallel series, which endows them with a new and richer meaning:

Mientras por competir con tu cabello
oro bruñido al sol relumbra en vano;
mientras con menosprecio en medio el llano
mira tu blanca frente el lilio bello;
　mientras a cada labio, por cogello,
siguen más ojos que al clavel temprano,
y mientras triunfa con desdén lozano
del luciente cristal tu gentil cuello,
　goza cuello, cabello, labio y frente,
antes que lo que fue en tu edad dorada
oro, lilio, clavel, cristal luciente,
　no sólo en plata o vïola troncada
se vuelva, mas tú y ello juntamente
en tierra, en humo, en polvo, en sombra, en nada.

While in competing with your hair,
Burnished gold shines in the sun in vain,
While with disdain your white forehead
Looks at the fair lily in the midst of the plain;

> While more eyes follow each lip, to seize it,
> Than follow the early carnation,
> And while with spirited scorn your lovely
> Neck triumphs over gleaming crystal;
>   Rejoice in your neck, hair, lip and forehead,
> Before what in your golden age
> Was gold, lily, carnation, gleaming crystal,
>   Not only turns to silver or becomes like a violet cut down,
> But you and all this together are reduced to
> Earth, smoke, dust, shadow, nothing.

Now the construction of the *Lazarillo* follows a very similar pattern. The various stages in the previous history of the town crier act like a set of conditional clauses, directed (often explicitly, as we have seen in the adventures with the blind man) towards a future which is to fill them with meaning. Each one of these stages, closely connected to the others,[27] adds new elements that progressively define the personality of the protagonist, channelling all this material towards the denouement. And here, from a new perspective, the principal elements in the structure are reviewed as they are juxtaposed, almost by surprise, with a series of facts which prove to be a natural extension of those elements and which, in turn, fully bring out their semantic and structural meaning.

The fact is that the entire novel displays the same unity of direction that we pointed out in the prophecy of the blind man, in the appeals to His Worship or in the coincidences between the opening and the conclusion.[28] As a child, Lázaro spends his first twelve short years, under Antona Pérez's protection, sheltered from the world, in a state of 'naïveté' ('simpleza'): twelve years that are dismissed in a few paragraphs because the narrator, 'like a child', spent them 'asleep' (p. 67); and it is precisely those events picked out here (the persecutions 'por justicia', associating with 'good people', Zaide's comings and goings . . .) which reappear at the end, now transformed into elements in 'the case'. By contrast, quite a number of carefully contrived pages are devoted to the short period spent with the blind man. The 'almost six months' in Maqueda in the service of an avaricious priest merit a whole chapter to themselves: Lázaro, who by now is alert and on his guard, after the lessons he learned with his first master, fights valiantly for his life; and his hunger in chapter 2 will be fully satisfied in chapter 7: the loaves of good bread that the priest from Maqueda received in the church as offerings and which he refused to give to Lázaro (the motif around which the entire episode revolves) are (and are not) the same loaves that Lázaro mentions in connection with the Archpriest of San Salvador's generous gifts. The two months with the squire (chapter 3) first teach the boy the emptiness and hypocrisy of the prevailing view of honour; Lázaro has a soft spot for the squire, but when he finds himself confronted by 'the case' his behaviour is the exact opposite of his former master's: he sacrifices his 'pride' and his good name to 'necessity',[29] for the sake of a quiet life. Finally, his three months in the service of the pardoner (chapter 5) confirm another important lesson: keeping quiet and staying out of the way when it suits him, saying nothing when this is to his advantage. This is perhaps why Lázaro confines himself to the role of narrator in this chapter, rather than the active character he was before;[30] thus during the period of his 'prosperity', Lázaro knows enough to stay out of trouble and 'avoid mentioning the subject' (p. 144) to his wife, and he becomes the very model of those 'Carthusian husbands' (as they were called because of their silence).[31] In this way, Lázaro de Tormes, town crier of Toledo, brings together and applies to 'the case' all the lessons he learned during his apprenticeship as a fully-grown man; and with this the span of the novel is finally closed and unified.

Illusionism

The medieval artist approaches reality through tradition. Tradition provides him with the fundamental patterns – the iconographical archetypes, let us say – with which to represent a subject, and confines direct, personal observation to points of detail. The literature of the period conforms to the same rule; realism here is usually concentrated on particulars to the same extent that it is absent from the nucleus of the plot. The Renaissance, on the other hand, according to Erwin Panofsky, holds that *la bona sperienza* is the foundation, the origin of the artist's task; the discovery of the vanishing point in perspective, in particular, confirms a new situation in which a work of art is no longer the result of mere obedience to a traditional code, and comes to be understood as 'a segment of the universe as it is observed – or, at least, as it could be observed – by a particular person from a particular point of view at a particular moment'.[32]

This definition fits the *Lazarillo* admirably. Our novel, too, rejects traditional preconceptions – the fixed and immutable pattern of things[33] – and conceives of reality as something variable, in terms of a particular point of view. It is worth recalling that the autobiographical vehicle of the letter allowed the author to smuggle the lowly subject of the *Lazarillo* in surreptitiously, by giving it an appearance of historicity and of belonging to a familiar literary genre, as contemporary orthodoxy demanded; but the use of the epistolary form, given the nature of the content, required a pretext in turn. We know this pretext only too well: Lázaro writes to explain 'the case'; 'the case' explains what Lázaro writes and how he writes it. The logical implications had to be followed through: if 'the case' was what provided a realistic motivation for the town crier to narrate his life history, then it also had to govern the selection and organization of the autobiographical material. Thus the novel was presented in terms of a point of view: that of the adult Lázaro[34] at the time of 'the case'.

I used the word *realistic*. The winds of truth were sweeping across Europe's intellectual landscape in the mid-sixteenth century. A new thirst for authenticity shook classical studies, historiography and beliefs out of their settled orthodoxy ... In the field of imaginative literature, the great undertaking of the humanists and the beneficiaries of humanism lay in creating a 'feigned' reality 'that has the colour of truth, even though it is not true', as Torres Naharro puts it;[35] the main priority was now to be verisimilitude ('Verisimilitude ... is the mean between fantastic fiction and the strictest truth', as Coluccio Salutati was already teaching,[36] and as the *Poetics* of Aristotle would confirm)[37] – invention subordinated to reason and experience. Doubtless the author of the *Lazarillo* shared such an ideal. Perhaps it was a desire for realism that prompted him to adopt an autobiographical form; perhaps it was a predilection for autobiography (as well as his whole worldview) that guided him towards realism. There is no way of finding out. In any case, *a posteriori*, each involved the other, and logical consistency was again inescapable: the entire novel had to be completely faithful to the autobiographical illusion; the only way the world could enter into it was through Lázaro's and Lazarillo's senses.

This is illustrated with particular clarity by an extreme situation in chapter 2. Lázaro sleeps with the key to the chest in his mouth,[38] 'in such a way and in such a position that the air I breathed out', he says, 'escaped through the hollow part of the key, which was made out of a tube, and whistled' (p. 97). The priest wakes up, thinks he can hear the 'whistling of the snake' that has been raiding his store of bread, locates it in the straw where Lazarillo is sleeping, and decides there and then to do away with the wretched creature: and so 'raising his stick right up in the air, thinking that it was directly below and that he would give it such a blow as to kill it', what he actually manages to do is to smash his poor servant's head in, leaving him unconscious for three days.

Fine. But did we not agree that Lázaro was asleep? Then where does he get all the details that make this scene so unforgettable? The narrator, with impeccable artistry, presents them sometimes as hypotheses which seem well-founded, judging by known causes and effects; sometimes as events narrated by the evil priest; and sometimes, more subtly, as a combination of his own guesses and information from other people: 'When he heard that he had hit me, for *I must have* yelled out at this vicious blow, *he said* that he had approached me ...' ('Como sintió que me había dado, según *yo debía* hacer gran sentimiento con el fiero golpe, *contaba él* que se había llegado a mí ...', p. 97). Lázaro is extremely careful to separate what is certain from what is in doubt, repeatedly using the conjectural '*must have* ...'.[39] But he still feels obliged to indicate the source of his information unequivocally: 'What happened during those next three days I cannot say, because I spent them in the whale's belly, as it were. But [I can say] that what I've just related is what I heard my master tell at length, after I regained consciousness, to everyone who came around' (p. 98). And so as not to leave a single loose end, he doubly underlines the starting point of his deductions (thereby confirming that they are just that): 'I began to get concerned about myself, and seeing what a sorry state I was in, instantly *suspected* the cause of my suffering' (p. 98).

This, of course, is the most obvious of the ways in which consistency with the point of view that informs the whole book is maintained. But, in addition, the particular nature of this perspective is frequently highlighted through the detailed reconstruction of the actual process of Lázaro's perception (rather than just the presentation of its results). It is worth remembering that the act of writing the novel itself constitutes a particular moment in its own plot. In an analogous and complementary manner, Lázaro the author records both what was perceived by Lázaro the protagonist and, in addition, the very act of perception. In this respect the third chapter – with its superb presentation of the figure of the squire, revealed in a slow, ironic manner, almost minute by minute, so that the reader may experience each episode with Lázaro – is perhaps one of the greatest achievements in the history of narrative art.[40]

Let us reread just the first few pages. Lazarillo and his new master, 'a squire, reasonably well dressed, well groomed', are walking along the streets of Toledo one summer morning. The boy has only just been taken on and as yet he knows nothing of his master: the latter's dress and bearing, however, seem to indicate that Lázaro is on to a good thing. They leave the market squares behind and Lázaro happily assumes: 'Perhaps he doesn't see anything he likes here ... he probably wants us to buy food somewhere else' (p. 102); later on an even more favourable indication is added to this assumption when the boy realizes that they have not actually been looking for food at all: 'I thought that my new master must be a man who bought food in bulk' (p. 103).[41]

The two of them walk around until eleven, enter the cathedral – 'I *saw him* hear mass, very devoutly', Lázaro remembers – and when they leave, they march off 'at a good pace ... down a street' (later the narrator will simply speak of 'going up *the* street' or '*my* street'): the boy is the 'happiest person in the world', imagining 'that by now lunch would be ready'. The clock is just striking one when they arrive 'at a house' – Lázaro is not yet in a position to say 'home': he is unaware that this house is going to be his own –

'in front of which my master stopped, and I with him' ('ante la cual mi amo se paró, y yo con él'). The narrator does not write 'we stopped': he distinguishes very precisely between the moment when the squire stops, and the moment when the boy notices this and stops too. The squire opens the door, revealing a 'dark, gloomy entrance', removes and folds his cloak with infinite care and enquires of Lázaro 'where I was from and how I had happened to arrive in that city'. The servant satisfies his curiosity with whatever lies seem most appropriate, wanting to finish quickly in order to lay the table and serve the stew. Conversation stops, the clock strikes two, and Lazarillo begins to get really worried: he remembers with alarm that the door was closed, that he has not seen 'a living soul in the house', that there is not even any furniture... The squire's question jolts him out of his thoughts: 'Have you eaten, boy?' (p. 104). And when Lázaro replies in the negative, the squire's very next remark ends all hope: 'You'll have to manage as best you can for now, and we'll have dinner later'.

The words ring like a knell in Lázaro's ears: he suddenly realizes that his third master is at least as stingy about satisfying his servant's hunger as his first two masters were; that the promising indications he saw when they first met – the lack of attention to 'bread and other provisions' (p. 102) – are in reality a sign of avarice or poverty. Later his doubts will be fully dispelled as other aspects of the squire are gradually revealed, with equal technical brilliance. But for the moment Lazarillo has discovered the main point: he will have to stay hungry. Suddenly everything makes sense: the closed door (a sign of a house without servants), the bare rooms, the silence ... the details which were neutral, indifferent, ignored up till this point, are now fully present in Lázaro's consciousness. In the 'light of hunger' (p. 92), they have acquired their true significance. The reader has shared in the protagonist's first innocent glances, has been mistaken like him, and like him, has been surprised when he understood the real meaning of the elements in the scene, all together and each separately.

The main lesson of such a mode of narration, as far as our present enquiry is concerned,[42] would seem to be epistemological in its implications. It is the self that gives the world its true reality: things and actions have no meaning in themselves – and therefore in a certain sense they have no existence – until the individual assimilates them; the world, devoid of meaning or endowed with all possible meanings (whichever you like), is modified to the same extent and at the same time as the individual.[43] The use of the third person in the novel (the form favoured by the invisible and omnipresent God with whom Flaubert identified the artist) often presupposes the existence of a stable and unambiguous universe, whose consistency and meaning are laid down once and for all.[44] The first person, by contrast, often tends to render reality problematic, projecting back on to it the uncertainty with which man confronts it, and, in the process, humanizing it.[45]

This is certainly what happens in this work. Implicitly, and yet not so implicitly, the narrative technique becomes an integral part of a worldview (that of the protagonist, of course; but also perhaps that of the real author?); and, moreover, it also becomes an integral part of the ultimate theme of the novel. For the child Lázaro reports only what he sees and hears, and confers reality and meaning on this only in so far as it affects him. But surely this is precisely what the adult Lázaro does with 'the case'. Why should the town crier admit what malicious gossips tell him about his wife, if he has not seen it, or if it happened – as he points out – 'before she married me' (p. 144)? He can only judge on the basis of visible effects: 'the truth' of the matter is not to be found in the rumours, nor in the behaviour of his wife, but in Lázaro himself. His smashed head was his proof of the priest of Maqueda's cruelty; the real meaning of the squire's indifference at the market stalls was determined by the fact that Lázaro went hungry all day; the 'prosperity' that he now enjoys is the most reliable evidence he could have of the good behaviour of his wife and the Archpriest. As the latter explains: 'Don't pay attention to what people say, but only to what affects you'. Excellent advice – like the person who gives it – but unnecessary: Lázaro has never done anything else.

The 'illusionistic presentation',[46] through which the reader shares the character's experiences, and, like him, is tricked or confused, is intensified in the second half of the novel. The third chapter applies the same masterly formula, that we identified in its introduction, to the whole of the two months Lázaro spends with the squire. The fifth chapter drives the point home thoroughly. Here Lázaro serves a pardoner and records the miracle to which his master resorts in order to prove the authority of his bulls and sell them. A false miracle, of course, but Lázaro narrates it – from the preparations right through to the consequences – as ingenuously as any of the deluded villagers might have done so: he is as surprised as the rest of the spectators ('Hearing us all shouting and making a noise . . .' p. 132); he does not question even for a moment the reality of what he is witnessing, nor does he indulge in any irony. In short, he is as 'amazed . . . as many other people' (p. 138). Only afterwards, seeing the pardoner and his accomplice laugh and joke about it all, does he discover the key to the 'miracle': 'I realized how the whole thing had been schemed by my scheming, inventive master; and although I was only a boy, I found it very funny' (p. 138). Once again, a whole episode has been split into two stages: a first stage of pure perception, so to speak, and a second stage in which the protagonist discovers an additional element which changes the meaning of the scene, by endowing it with a different sort of reality.

Such a technique, as I have said, dominates the narrative particularly from the opening of the third chapter onwards, and it enables the author to give us practice in the type of reading that will make the conclusion fully comprehensible, and tie together all the separate strands of the novel.[47] For Lázaro, as we have already indicated, structures his *Life* in the same way as he presents his meeting with the squire or the pardoner's miracle: throughout the book he provides information which is interesting in itself; and, in the last chapter, he introduces a new element – 'the case' – which gives a different meaning to all the material presented up to that moment.[48] The town crier reassesses his past and assimilates it in a new light, in exactly the same way as Lazarillo, on the basis of an analogous experience, reinterprets what he had previously perceived quite ingenuously: the mode of narration is a microcosm of the overall design. Thus the process of conceiving and executing the novel as point of view is fully realized on every level. And those elements which appeared to be mere conventional formulae (appealing to His Worship, for example, as one would in a letter) are shown to be rich in biographical substance (the writing of such a letter is itself an episode in Lázaro's life); whereas those elements to which one would initially ascribe a purely autonomous value are now revealed as being full of structural significance, in so far as they are seen to be subordinated to a unifying design.

The Chinese puzzle

In *The Life of Lazarillo*, as in Ortega y Gasset's *The Theme of Our Time*, 'perspective is one of the components of reality'.[49] Lázaro is constantly putting us on the alert by the very manner in which he narrates his story: the world does not have just one meaning; values exist only in relation to the individual and even then, they are only provisional. The style, of course, is fully consistent with the narrative conception. The different, even contradictory facets which objects present are as numerous as the stages through which the protagonist passes: the little jug that first delights Lázaro and then brains him is 'that bitter and sweet jug' ('aquel dulce y amargo jarro', p. 72); the six months spent in the service of the avaricious priest are – in the words of the town crier – 'the time I lived with him, or rather, died with him' ('el tiempo que con él viví o, por mejor decir, morí', p. 86). And, naturally, there are as many definitions of things and persons as there are individuals connected with them: the beggar with whom Lázaro starts out is 'my new and old master' ('mi nuevo y viejo amo', p. 66); at night the priest of Maqueda pursues 'the serpent, or young *sir*-pent' ('la culebra o culebro', p. 96) that has been rifling his bread store.[50] The language of the book captures the polysemy of life in a delightfully mischievous way, making use, for instance, of comparative expressions, the interpretation of which varies according to the point of view to which one relates them: Antona Pérez is confident that Lazarillo will turn out 'no ... worse' (p. 66) than his father (that is, 'as good' or 'as bad' as he); the Archpriest's mistress is 'as good a woman as any living within the gates of Toledo' – she is like all the rest or they are like her.

Since objects, and especially accepted moral standards, are so ambiguous, so relative for Lázaro, how are we to react when he invites us to find 'something good' ('algún fruto', p. 61) in the novel? How are we to interpret the lessons of Toledo's town crier? Can we take them to have any validity for people other than Lázaro himself? Or are they non-transferable, like season tickets?

Let us consider an example. If there is an explicit 'thesis' in the novel, it consists in 'showing what a virtue it is for lowly people to manage to rise; and what a vice for the high-born to let themselves fall' ('mostrar cuánta virtud sea saber los hombres subir, siendo bajos; y dejarse bajar, siendo altos, cuánto vicio', p. 68). Lázaro puts it as clearly as one could possibly wish: he has written about 'the case' so as to give us a picture of himself 'and also so that those who have inherited noble estates should consider how little credit is due to them, for Fortune favoured them, and how much more those men achieved who, despite hostile Fortune, have reached a safe harbour by dint of rowing hard and skilfully' (p. 62).

This idea would have struck traditionally minded people as outrageous.[51] Throughout the Middle Ages, in fact, a very different doctrine had been gaining acceptance: society is an exact reflection of the cosmic order and of the Kingdom of God.[52] Social classes, then, are as immutable and immovable as the orbits of the planets and the ascending order of the choirs of angels: any attempt to change one's status, to move up the hierarchy, implies rebelling against natural law and Divine Providence, which – as Don Juan Manuel, for example, puts it – amounts to a direct route to damnation, for 'social estates are so manifold and various that what is appropriate to one is highly damaging to another'.[53] One must therefore, as Juan de Santa María explains, submit to destiny which has fixed for 'each person a position, his place in society and specific jurisdictional limits for the occupation with which he will be entrusted, without even considering that this will ever be changed or altered'.[54]

But around 1554 not everyone was taken in by these orthodox ideas. An important humanist faction argued strongly for the opposite view: that (in the words of Pero Mexía) 'wherever man is born, he is entitled to try to achieve greatness and renown, as long as he follows the path of virtue'.[55] Inheritance and Fortune, according to this new way of thinking, have no power against virtue and personal effort. As Leonardo Bruni puts it, in a memorable early formulation, 'Everyone enjoys the same liberty...; everyone has the same prospect of attaining honour and reaching a high position, as long as he is industrious, and naturally able, and leads a serious-minded and respectable life; for what our city [Florence] requires of its citizens is virtue and integrity. Whoever possesses these qualities is considered sufficiently noble to participate in the government of the republic ...'[56] And the opposite also holds good: whoever does not possess them is of no merit or worth, however illustrious his lineage: 'Slothful, indolent, wicked and perverse people', asserts Poggio Bracciolini, 'who assume they will succeed their forbears, are to be held in lesser esteem than other people according to how far they fall short of the example set by those from whom they are descended'.[57]

These two antithetical positions were set up against each other time and time again. They had already been contrasted thus in some famous *Invectivae* of doubtful authenticity, in which 'Sallust alleged that Tully [Cicero] came from low, obscure stock and from humble parents of little worth, and for this reason he should be despised', whereas 'Tully contradicted him by saying that his own virtuous actions had brought him to the position he held, and that for this reason he was worthy of even more honour than those who had inherited it from their ancestors'.[58] Later, a very popular *Disputatio de nobilitate* (by Buonaccorso da Montemagno, 1428) had marked the beginning of an endless flood of treatises and dialogues that argued both sides of the question. Throughout the fifteenth and sixteenth centuries the debate continued with an intensity which did not diminish even for a moment.

And Lázaro is certainly quite willing to join in the argument. Explicitly, I insist, he sides with the innovative faction and affirms that his life shows 'what a virtue it is to manage to rise'. Indeed, he has become the protagonist in 'the case' thanks to his 'ability and respectable way of life', and as such, does he not enjoy 'every favour and assistance' (p. 142), does he not find himself in a state of 'prosperity and at the height of all good fortune' (p. 144)? Of course no one in Spain at the time of Charles V could admit seriously that to rise from being the son of a thieving miller and laundry woman (concubine of a *morisco*) to being a town crier[59] and husband of a sacrilegious adultress constituted any real advance. The reader knows that Lázaro, whatever he may say, has not risen. He has not risen because, despite his assertions, he has not really practised 'virtue'. And with this, *ex contrario*, Lázaro's declaration of principles (which is very much the same as those of Pero Mexía, Leonardo Bruni or the Cicero of the *Invectivae* I have cited) is resolutely confirmed: virtue is the means by which men rise in the world, a humanist of the new type would argue; Lázaro has not exercised it properly, *ergo* he has not risen.[60]

But let us reconsider the matter from the perspective which Juan Manuel, Juan de Santa María or the pseudo-Sallust would have adopted. The essential point is still the same: Lázaro has not risen. Why not? The conservative mentality has its answers ready to hand: because bad character is inherited; because to aspire to change one's position in society is always intrinsically sinful; because the 'virtue' of anyone who attempts to do so is really a cover for the worst sort of 'vice'. *The Life of Lazarillo de Tormes* also confirms class prejudice and ridicules those who denigrate it: only a scoundrel like Lázaro – a reader firmly placed within the establishment would argue – could maintain 'how little credit is due' to 'those who inherited noble estates'; and his form of 'safe harbour' is the only one that people with principles of that sort can ever reach.

There remains a third solution, one perfectly consistent with the narrative and linguistic technique of making the only positive reality of the object depend on the subject: namely that Lázaro *has* risen; that for a poor wretch like him, leaving the hunger of the road for the modest 'prosperity' of an 'office under the crown' really does amount to some sort of progress – especially when other possibilities of advancement are revealed: 'my master has promised me that which I trust he will fulfil' (p. 143). And if this is so, then innovators and traditionalists are both wrong and right at the same time: wrong, because it actually is possible to 'rise' despite lack of 'virtue' and despite one's birth; and right, because it is possible to 'rise' only to Lázaro's level. It is pointless, then, to attempt to establish any norm other than a purely subjective one:

no theoretical guidelines can take account of men's inexhaustible variety and complexity.

We have come full circle: the individual is the only effective criterion of truth. The most widely canvassed principles and accepted contemporary standards of behaviour can equally easily be affirmed or denied. There are no values: there are only lives, and what holds good for one life may be quite inapplicable to another. That seems to be the lesson Lázaro offers us.

But let us follow this lesson through, and we may then find ourselves unable to accept it: such inconclusiveness is a consequence of the strict novelization of point of view. We are up against the old problem of the metalogical paradox. 'We Cretans always lie.' Is this assertion from Epimenides true or false? Or then again: 'Everything is relative.' Does this apply even to such a proposition itself? 'Values exist only in relation to the individual' is what Lázaro is ultimately telling us (in the only language in which it can be said – actions). In that case, should this hypothesis be taken to apply only to our town crier? And if so, will the idea be totally vitiated by the fact that it comes from a scoundrel? Does the 'something good' to be found in the novel simply amount to showing the kind of distortion of which a depraved mentality is capable?[61]

One could legitimately argue that it does, though it is not necessary to do so. We already know how the Lazarillo is constructed. A particular point of view selects the subject matter, establishes the overall structure, determines the narrative technique and controls the style; and, in turn, subject matter, structure, technique and style serve to elucidate this point of view. As in one of those Chinese puzzles which consist of progressively smaller boxes one inside the other, all the elements which make up the *Lazarillo* are homologous, and strike one as images of each other. In the final analysis, they are all images of 'the case': the duality of the 'bitter and sweet jug', for example, prefigures the final duality of the protagonist himself ('I don't know what and I do know what'; 'no sé qué y sí sé qué'); the two stages in the presentation of the false miracle foreshadow the two stages in the town crier's self-revelation, and so on and so forth. Now if the author's aim was to discredit the protagonist completely, then the admirable structure outlined above would be nothing more than an elaborate psychological experiment undertaken in support of a modest premiss: 'Only someone as absurd and systematically perverse as Lázaro could ridicule the great ideals of virtue and honour.' But would this not mean that a disproportionate amount of effort, and an ambiguity which has incomprehensibly been left without any explicit caveat, have been directed to the defence of a banal and wholly uncontroversial thesis? Or perhaps, given that this thesis was so well known and so unexceptionable, it could safely be ignored, and perhaps the centre of interest was supposed to be the comic virtuosity with which all the threads of the narrative were gradually being woven together?

While we are following this line of thought, it is worth asking ourselves whether that may actually have been the author's sole purpose: namely to present a superb example of comic craftsman-ship, quite independent of any more or less didactic implications. The monotonously committed literature of more recent times has perhaps dulled our sense of humour, and, moreover, it has perhaps made us forget that the mechanisms of laughter do not work the same way in fiction as in life. The *Lazarillo* – and it is high time this was said – is a tremendously funny book; and as such it obeys the law of humorous coherence ('la "vérité" facétieuse', as the great Marcel Bataillon calls it)[62] which tends to create an autonomous universe, a universe where all that counts is wit, surprise, and the linking together of amusing incidents, and in which ethical imperatives and social conventions are suspended. When Lázaro *kills* (or almost kills) the blind man, we laugh[63] instead of feeling outraged (as we presumably would in real life). Is this all the author was aiming to do, to make us laugh and nothing more?

I find this explanation very congenial, but not entirely satisfac-tory. Sometimes the very mention of a theme forces us to adopt a certain attitude towards it. 'For in that series of acts that con-stitute the network of "what happens"', again in the words of Marcel Bataillon, 'there are many that cannot be articulated without being qualified by at least implicit reference to the norms and values of a given society.'[64] Consider again the problem raised above. 'None of those great ideals that society proclaims amounts

to anything except in so far as it affects me', we thought we heard
Lázaro say as we saw him ignore both Cicero and Sallust. But is
this because of the ideals or because of him? What is the
'something good' he promises us? Is the underlying thesis (1) the
product of a perverse outlook, (2) merely a humorous pose, or (3)
an adequate response to a multivalent reality, resolved as no more
than a series of points of view?

My own preference is for this third hypothesis. The Chinese
puzzle of our novel – the flawlessly coherent interdependence of
all its components – fits together too well to be regarded merely as
a cleverly contrived fiction: Lázaro's relativism cannot be entirely
artificial; the author must have shared it to a considerable extent.
Multiple meanings, ambiguity and irony seem to me such essential and pervasive features of the *Lazarillo*[65] that I can only explain
them to myself as products of a thoroughgoing scepticism
(towards the affairs of this world, not the next)[66] as to the
possibility of man knowing reality – of 'knowing the truth for
certain, and quickly', as Cervantes was to put it[67] (and there, in
my opinion, was a mind closely akin to that of our anonymous
author, if ever there was one). The self is the only guide we have in
the confusing jungle of the world: but we should not forget that it
is a partial and momentary guide, as variable as the world itself;
and that, by definition, it is impossible to derive from it any firm
conclusions, particularly in the sphere of values, that may lay
claim to universal validity.

Such an interpretation does not undermine the second hypothesis in any really decisive way (on the contrary, humour has
always been a closer ally of sceptics than of dogmatists); and,
moreover, it leaves the cornerstone of the first hypothesis intact: it
does not deny that Lázaro may be a scoundrel if he is looked at in
terms of conventional standards, but it does caustically undermine those standards themselves. The author appreciates his
character's reasons, understands his essential truth (it is impossible to take seriously – let alone to regard as definitive – the
principles pompously aired by spokesmen of any shade of
opinion) and reveals the meaninglessness of the rigid value
judgements which prevailed at the time. And this also gives rise to
the rich and ironic characterization of the protagonist, ingenuous

and cunning, charitable and cruel, all light and shade (and not all light or all dark, as one might expect to find in an unambiguous *roman à thèse* of the period).

But I would go even further than this: if my reading of the *Lazarillo* is correct, I think that the work's very existence becomes considerably more comprehensible. Relativism, in value theory as in epistemology, is also a type of humanism. Lázaro's fortunes and misfortunes seem to teach us that 'there are no values: there are only lives – individuals'. But surely this attention to individuality constitutes the hallmark of the modern novel as created by a Cervantes or a Fielding. Implicit in this recognition of subjectivity as a measure of all things stirs a truly novelistic impulse which the anonymous author of the *Lazarillo* must have found very attractive. After all, if the servant's self has as much value in the final analysis as the master's, why should the lowly figure of the town crier not be of interest, even if literary tradition thought otherwise? If the self is the touchstone of reality, what form could be more realistic than autobiography?

2

The life and opinions of Guzmán de Alfarache

You must have a little patience. I have undertaken, you see, to write not only my life, but my opinions also, hoping and expecting that your knowledge of my character, and of what kind of a mortal I am, by the one, would give you a better relish for the other... Then nothing that has touched me will be thought trifling in its nature, or tedious in its telling.

Tristram Shandy

Intention and construction

We make no claims here to originality. The most third-rate histories of literature and the most execrable popular encyclopedias generally point out quite correctly (even if they get nothing else right) the one essential fact needed for a proper understanding of *La vida de Guzmán de Alfarache, atalaya de la vida humana* (The Life of Guzmán de Alfarache, Watchtower of Human Life) (1599–1604): namely that the account of the protagonist's adventures, placed in the mouth of Guzmán himself, is not a continuous, uninterrupted stream but is interspersed at every stage with sermons, *moralités*, theoretical meditations; in short, that the narrative pure and simple is punctuated by a whole string of non-narrative disquisitions that we would nowadays call *essays*, but in an earlier age were usually referred to as *discourses*.[1] As I say, literary primers and cheap handbooks register this fact quite accurately – but then go on immediately to misinterpret it, evaluating only the *factual* content (events, anecdotes, Guzmán's vicissitudes) and ignoring the rest as hypocritical 'digressions' (for the censor's eye), excrescences of a medieval tradition, or, at best, an unfortunate mistake on the part of Mateo Alemán, mere dead wood in the overall fiction.

This inability to do justice to *Guzmán de Alfarache* in its entirety, and to interpret the book as it actually stands, without arbitrarily mutilating it, rests on a poor application of the concept of the *novel* (and on various romantic fallacies which will not concern us here). It so happens that *The Life of Guzmán* is undoubtedly a novel, but it corresponds only in part to what is popularly regarded as the archetype of the genre, established in the nineteenth century by the efforts of a few geniuses and a great many hack writers of cheap serial novels: the novel as pure story and description, unencumbered by philosophical reflections, explicit opinions and overtly didactic accretions. And since the only critical categories available to exponents of the usual approach are those designed to cope with the most obvious manifestations of such an archetype, they are obliged, when they come up against the *Watchtower of Human Life* and find it categorized as a novel, to give up any attempt to explain it as a whole. Certainly they can arbitrarily extract everything they consider to be narrative material and subject it to the usual nineteenth-century critical canons; at best, they can extol the splendid style of the 'digressions'; but they hardly ever manage to appreciate that if Mateo Alemán wrote one book, and not two, it was because he considered that all the component parts were well integrated: and that the function of the critic is not to salvage the narrative material and declare the 'digressions' to be irrelevant, but rather to highlight the connecting factor which integrates them (without being so naïve as to suppose that it is limited to the actual binding).

Enrique Moreno Báez, in an indispensable monograph,[2] was the first critic in modern times to apply himself seriously to this task; and he was quick to recognize such a connecting factor precisely where obstinately anachronistic commentators had refused to see anything more than empty verbiage and lame excuses: in the author's explicitly didactic intentions. The fact is that Mateo Alemán repeatedly states[3] that he wrote the work out of a 'desire to be useful' ('celo de aprovechar', I, preliminaries; p. 93),[4] concerned 'only with the common good' (p. 94). The numerous declarations of exemplary intention, however, would mean nothing if they were not backed up by a dazzling display of a whole range of artistic procedures, whose full value cannot be perceived unless they are examined in the light of that didactic aim. Because despite all the trivial, facile arguments about the 'Intentional Fallacy', it is impossible to approach a literary work without bearing the author's explicit aims in mind, just as it is absurd to criticize any artefact for failing to serve a purpose for which it was never designed. Only when one realizes that *Guzmán de Alfarache* is not the product of a purely fictional intention (of the sort that actuated Balzac or Eugène Sue), but rather of a wider-ranging educational aim (which essentially uses the novel as its vehicle, to be sure, but also makes use of other genres familiar in the period: the *silva*, or miscellany, for example)[5] can one do full justice to Alemán's great work. And paradoxically, only then is it possible to appreciate its strict uniqueness as a novel, and thus to observe that whereas on the one hand the *pícaro*'s adventures also function as sermons (directly or *ex contrario*, by presenting positive or negative examples), so too do the most important overt sermons also function as adventures, for they are an integral part of the portrait of the protagonist. Of course, the second of these types of fusion is inseparable from the fact that the *Guzmán* is presented to us in the form of an autobiography, and within this framework every element is turned into fiction. The fundamental key to the work, in my opinion, is simply this: that Alemán conceived it, on every level, as the particular point of view of the fictional narrator and character.

This does not mean that the real author did not share the ideas expressed by his creation, at least for the most part (we already know what a difficult question this is when it arises in the *Lazarillo*). It simply means that he strove to make the worldview articulated in the book correspond in every particular to the disposition of its hero; that he made it arise in an entirely coherent manner from the whole course of his life, with the precision of a 'poetic construct'.[6] (If anyone imagines for a moment that this is true of all autobiographical fiction, let him read the apocryphal *Second Part of the Life of the Rogue* by 'Mateo Luján de Sayavedra', if he has the endurance.) Consider, for instance, the fact that by the authority of an illustrious tradition, the examination of man's dignity and of his misery were regarded as quite compatible:[7] it was therefore possible, for example, to sing the praises of the intellect on one page and take stock of its failings on the next, without the slightest contradiction. By the same token, there is nothing surprising in the fact that Alemán should have paid elaborate tribute to reason and the senses one moment, and heaped opprobrium on them the next. But what does need pointing out, having established that he accepted both positions, is that he included the tribute in his carefully composed biography of St Anthony of Padua (Seville, 1604; II, x) and reserved the opprobrium for *Guzmán de Alfarache* (II, i, 3; p. 508): indeed, the latter, rather than the former, seemed appropriate coming from the protagonist of this work.

One character in search of an author

Some readers will doubtless remember the protagonist in question. Guzmán 'himself writes his life history from the galleys, to which he has been condemned for crimes he committed, having been a very skilful thief' (I, preliminaries; p. 96). But before ending up in this position he has had a positively protean career. The orphaned son of more than one father, he is twelve years old when he decides to try his luck away from Seville, his home town, 'commending myself', he says, 'to God and good people, in whom I put my trust' (I, i, 2; p. 145). But right from his very first encounters with them, in disreputable roadside inns, he is forced to abandon this naïve confidence in his fellow men. As a servant boy in a hostelry on his way to court, an errand boy and a scullion in Madrid, Guzmanillo becomes inured to a life of evil, ignoring the continual reproaches of his conscience. One stroke of luck (two and a half thousand *reales* stolen from an unwary victim) and he is off to Italy, under the aegis of a company of soldiers and in the service of their captain. In Genoa he seeks the friendship and protection of some relatives, from whom, evil-looking devil that he is, all he receives is scorn and good cudgelling. As a beggar and a false cripple in Rome, he is taken in by a kind-hearted cardinal who employs him as a page and offers him not only an education but also every opportunity he could wish for to change his ways. Instead of doing so, he obstinately and impatiently leaves the Cardinal and becomes a cross between a secretary, a pimp, and a private buffoon to the French ambassador. Wounded pride (the whole city laughed at one of his grotesque misfortunes) makes him leave Rome, and Guzmanillo decides to settle down. But after being robbed and finding himself destitute, he soon returns to his former bad habits (with the help of the hapless Sayavedra): the winnings from his card sharping and the proceeds of a highly ingenious swindle enable him to get to Genoa, now looking thoroughly respectable, win the esteem of the relatives who treated him so badly before, cheat them out of a fortune and take to his heels. (On the trip to Spain, incidentally, Sayavedra goes insane and throws himself into the sea.) Having settled at court, he marries, becomes a merchant, and gets involved in some shady dealings; his wife dies and he goes bankrupt at almost the same time, and Guzmán decides to make sure of having enough to eat, free himself from his creditors and change his ways, by the expedient of getting a theology degree at Alcalá de Henares and taking religious orders. He is barely a month away from achieving this when love crosses his path, and lures him into a foolish marriage with Gracia, an innkeeper's daughter. Guzmán soon takes the plunge, and having now become a 'Carthusian' husband (like Lazarillo de Tormes), he lives off his wife's charms. The couple wander through Alcalá, Madrid, and finally Seville, where Gracia escapes to Italy with a captain. 'Alone and poor', Guzmán 'starts thieving again as he used to' (II, iii, 6; p. 848), and when he attempts to go on to greater crimes, to try his luck as a big-time thief, 'he is arrested and condemned to the galleys for life' (II, iii, 7; p. 859). And there he is visited by divine grace: the galley slave purges his sins with tears, resolutely persists in living virtuously[8] and 'finally puts paid to the misfortunes of his evil life' (II, iii, 9; p. 905).

This summary is so bare that it may even be misleading. But let us agree to accept it for the moment as an expository device and, at the risk of exaggeration, highlight two distinct phases in Guzmán's career: a first period of action, with a highly active Guzmanillo as protagonist; and a second period of narration, in which the now sober, penitent Alfarache enumerates his past acts of villainy, interspersing them with moral reflections. Mateo Alemán himself actually made the distinction in the novel (I, preliminaries; p. 94) between the sphere of *conseja* (the story of Guzmán's life, essentially, together with other narrative material) and that of *consejo* (which, for our purposes, can be taken to mean 'opinions', an explicitly articulated doctrine). Now if the conversion introduces a disjunction between Guzmanillo and

Guzmán, between the actor and the author, one's first reaction is to ascribe sole responsibility for the entire mass of sermons and disquisitions to the latter. Thus the 'life' and 'opinions' (*conseja* and *consejo*) would ultimately be united in the figure of Guzmán. But such a union would be intolerably artificial, because, in fact, Guzmán the writer would then have nothing to do with Guzmán the character:[9] the final repentance would mean that the character of the *pícaro* has been seriously undermined for the sake of creating the thinnest of pretexts to justify the use of first-person narration.

But why, in that case, has the first person been used? If 'life' and 'opinions' were completely separate, why destroy the verisimilitude of the whole? It would have been easier for Alemán himself to assume directly the roles of narrator and moralist. He doubtless had good reasons for not doing so. Let us consider one fact (since we cannot consider all of them) which will help to make these reasons clearer to us. Most of the sermons can be attributed to the mature Guzmán, by now a 'perfect man' (II, prologue; p. 467), but there are some others, of a different aesthetic value, which are placed in the mouth or heart of the vacillating Guzmanillo.

In the first part, for instance, at the beginning of the second book, we find three whole chapters devoted essentially to a bitter denunciation 'of the vanity of honour' (I, ii, 4; p. 271). Guzmán had to abandon any claim to honour[10] during his trip to Madrid, as he resorted to begging and found himself obliged to sell, piece by piece, the clothes off his back, until he was left in his shirt and breeches. Once he is at court, in order to avoid suffering the punishment inflicted on vagabonds and to take advantage of the 'glorious freedom' (I, ii, 2; p. 259) associated with the job, he becomes an errand boy, the occupation most appropriate to members of the picaresque order and also the most dishonourable, according to contemporary opinion.[11] 'Not bothering about serving or being served' (I, ii, 4; p. 276), free from having to worry about what others think of him, and with his basic needs more or less satisfied, the boy comes to enjoy life as a messenger: in it he discovers the possibility of living a godly life by honestly carrying his 'burdens' ('cargos', I, ii, 3; p. 268) and ignoring 'the heavy burden that honour imposes' ('lo que carga el peso de la honra', I, ii, 2; p. 261). He keeps his eyes open to things around him, meditates on some words he heard from the pulpit (p. 266), reflects on an experience (p. 272), and reawakens his earlier religious upbringing; and this gives rise, in a perfectly natural way, to his long monologue against vain notions of honour.

This monologue, then, cannot be considered as a discourse extraneous to the plot, but rather forms an inseparable part of it: in short, it is one of the moments when Guzmán becomes self-conscious, and is inseparable from his concrete situation as an errand boy in Habsburg Madrid. He now chooses what had previously been imposed on him. Circumstances have led him to eschew honour; his observation and beliefs have helped him to rationalize his renunciation of it; and hence, his diatribes against that social evil are a fully consistent phase in his development as an individual.

But in these chapters, on the other hand, the reflections of Guzmán the *pícaro* interfere with the comments of Guzmán the galley slave. These two types of 'opinion', the judgments 'of the present and [those of] the past' (I, ii, 3; p. 268), are separate but complementary, each recognizable as a distinct current but both flowing towards the same point. Guzmanillo will later stumble and pick himself up again many times: he will fall again into the traps of honour, and each time he will manage, more or less successfully, to get out of them. The happy days when he dragged his basket round the plazuela de Santa Cruz, unconcerned about what people might say and set fair on a course of virtue, will not, however, be expunged from his memory: from Rome to the galleys, he will often look back on them nostalgically. The lesson learned on that occasion (and formulated in his uneasy 'soliloquy', I, ii, 4; p. 271) may not be followed by him most of the time, but it will always be in his mind, and above all, it will definitively materialize at the critical moment of conversion. By the same token, the narrator's denunciations of the chimera of honour are perfectly consistent with those of the protagonist: they signify precisely the culmination of one decisive episode in his story, the logical and well-motivated development of one facet of his personality.

This fact is extremely significant, it seems to me, and I think it brings us to the very heart of the problem. Guzmanillo's diatribes against honour – which, far from being irrelevant digressions, arise entirely naturally from the *pícaro*'s circumstances – explain the fact that eventually, after his conversion, Guzmán comes to deliver other similar diatribes; and, in the same way, a large proportion of young Guzmán's adventures makes it convincing that he should finally set himself up as a writer and accounts for the very existence of the novel in the particular form it adopts.

The most obvious feature in the portrayal of the transition from actor to author is the care with which the protagonist's studies and intellectual proclivities are specified. He is 'a man of clear intellect' (I, preliminaries; p. 96), whose intelligence and quick-wittedness are clearly displayed in a whole series of difficult situations, and who (like Cervantes) loves reading even old scraps of paper in the street (I, ii, 4; p. 272). Guzmán receives an excellent education (four hours a day – we may as well be precise because he himself is specific on this point) during his years at Rome in the service of the Cardinal (I, iii, 9; p. 428). And even if he quite soon reverts to evil he is not so wholehearted about it as not to be tempted, while passing through Bologna, by the idea of 'resuming my studies', as he himself says (II, ii, 2; p. 602). When things become difficult and bankruptcy looms, his one idea is to take advantage of his apprenticeship in 'humane letters' and read 'Arts and Theology' at the University of Alcalá (II, iii, 4; p. 798), and he tackles this task with such determination and relish that everyone – from the rector downwards – considers him 'one of the best students' (II, iii, 4; p. 817), certain to get a professorship before long.

What could be surprising, then, about the fact that the very moment of his conversion is explicitly interwoven with memories of what he had learned in the lecture theatre (II, iii, 8; p. 890)? This is so obvious that we might have left it unsaid (too obvious, some may think; even so, what is involved here is not just a facile device: it would only be so if it were not woven into a tight web of coincidental factors). But we have clear evidence of the importance that the subject held for Mateo Alemán. For the fact is that in his judgement of the apocryphal *Second Part of the Life of the Rogue*,

the point to which he devotes most attention is the unsuitability of
the 'discourses' that his imitator had ascribed to Guzmán;[12] and
the first and most serious criticism he levels at him regarding the
characterization of the protagonist is that he made him emerge
from Alcalá as 'such a lackadaisical individual and such a poor
logician [that] it amounted to *cutting the thread which holds together the
whole fabric of what was supposed to be demonstrated by recounting his life
history here*' (II, prologue; p. 467). What we are dealing with here is
not a mere detail, but the very essence of *Guzmán de Alfarache*, in its
entirety, as 'life' and as 'opinions'.

Between fears and hopes

A couple of trial borings from different levels have provided us
with confirmation of a single basic truth: the later Guzmán is
present in the earlier Guzmanillo; and it is correct to say that the
conversion separates them in a number of ways only if we also
point out that it unites them in just as many other ways. But there
is more to it than that: the transition from Guzmán the actor to
Guzmán the author is not only shown to be carefully motivated,
but also constitutes the true thematic core of the work. In the
latter, the various episodic nuclei are subordinated to one main
structural thread: the story of a conversion, the analysis of an
individual consciousness.

Alemán, of course, did not reduce the whole novel to this
inward exploration of his character's psyche. He had too clear an
appreciation that sinners do not read boring books (as my teacher
Martín de Riquer used to remind us), and that the medicine must
be 'covered over with something to make it look attractive' (II, iii,
3; p. 774). Using autobiography and turning the entire content of
the book into *fiction* – so as to make the generalized preaching part
of the process by which the protagonist is individualized – was a
decisive step towards arousing the reader's interest and also, of
course, reinforcing the various different arguments involved, by
presenting them as truths not merely asserted but *demonstrated* in
the experience of an individual. But this was clearly not enough
for the less well educated public. Alemán did not hesitate,
therefore, to include chapters or passages devoted to Guzmán's

'external' adventures – and he must have enjoyed writing them as much as we enjoy reading them. As a typical example one could cite the brilliant section (II, ii, 5 and 6) given over to the swindling of the Milanese merchant: the meticulousness of these pages, which show a close eye for detail and are directed to the exact reconstruction of each and every one of the circumstances of the swindle, is designed not so much to draw attention to the cleverness of the *pícaro* or his reversion to evil ways as to grip the reader in the same way that so many thrillers do today (or so many *libri vagatorum* did long ago): by concentrating on action, on exciting intrigue, on the sheer irresistible fascination of the plot.

I would almost go so far as to say that such moments of *superficial* narration are the real 'digressions' in the *Watchtower of Human Life*. Alemán (and this is the rule, not the exception) was capable of combining to perfection an extremely entertaining anecdote and a profound study of the hero, well-defined didactic interest and sound structural relevance. This could be demonstrated from a great many passages; suffice it here to refer the reader to a typical example: Guzmán's second visit to Genoa. For this reason we cannot help feeling slightly surprised when we come across an episode like the trick played on the Milanese, which is beautifully put together but adds very little to the creation of character. For in some ways the same is true of such fragments as of *novelle*, or other interludes which serve merely to entertain (the *Arancel de necedades*, for example): Alemán could have replaced them with other similar ones, within the limits of the protagonist's personality, or he could have put them in a different order quite freely, because they do not fulfil a sufficiently clear and specific structural function; they do not serve to articulate the story around the various pivotal points of the basic subject: Guzmán's spiritual development.

It is important to realize that the process of the *pícaro*'s conversion goes hand in hand with the gradual consolidation of the point of view that dominates the novel; and it constitutes, in terms of the ideology presented in the *Guzmán*, one of the most prominent motifs of the work. This process is a long and complex one and I do not propose to examine it at length here. I shall confine myself to a few observations. Let me first emphasize that, despite the usual tendency to exaggerate indiscriminately the gap between Guzmán and Guzmanillo, the division between them operates as much in a diachronic as in a synchronic dimension: as much longways as sideways.

Alemán makes us aware of this from the very outset of the action. When he has just run away from home, in fact, and is still a very short distance from Seville, Guzmán stops on the steps of a hermitage to think things over: 'There, for the first time, I took stock of my life and considered how it had progressed so far' (i, i, 3; p. 147), he tells us. This fact should not escape our notice. Guzmán's first concern, having only just left the nest, is to look at his past and at himself and examine his conscience: and that is also his concern at the end of his peregrination through life: to recall his early life, to make a 'general confession' (ii, i, 1; p. 484), that is, to write his autobiography. The real significance of this fact, highlighted by the prominent position in which it is introduced, seems obvious: Guzmán the author is organically continuous with Guzmán the actor.

But what concerns us now is the substance of the young fugitive's introspective reflections. Guzmanillo is uncertain, not knowing 'what to do or where to head for. What gave me courage on the one hand, terrified me on the other. I found myself caught between fears and hopes, a precipice before me and wolves behind. I wavered; I wanted to put it all in God's hands ...' (p. 147). Night falls, and with it the lad's imagination rests; but when he awakens the same uncertainty persists; 'I did not know where I was going; I had not noticed'; of the various possible paths, therefore, 'I took the one that looked most attractive, wherever it might lead' (p. 148).[13]

This, of course, is the old motif of Hercules at the crossroads, associated for centuries with the emblem of the pythagorean *Y*: 'representation of human life' (as Alemán himself explains in another work), whose 'stem or upright section' denotes 'the earliest part of our life, uncertain and unwilled, inclining neither one way nor the other', while the two branches above it, 'a narrow one on the right and a wide one on the left', proclaim 'what the Holy Gospel preaches to us today [Matthew 7. 14]: "Narrow is the way, which leadeth us unto the enjoyment of [eternal] life, and

broad that which leadeth us, through pleasure, to destruction'''.[14]
The beginning of the *pícaro*'s adventures is clearly symbolic –
Guzmán chooses the easier path and the sad consequences of this
choice follow all too soon. But its particular significance, for our
present purposes, is as a symptom of a fundamental feature of the
protagonist: brought up in a faith that has *all* the answers, certain
that *everything* comes down to a question of salvation or damnation, Guzmán suffers in the most acutely real way the tragic
impossibility of serving two masters.

He does indeed spend his days caught 'between fears and
hopes', 'wavering' between putting himself 'in God's hands' and
letting himself be carried along 'by the impetus of his own false
desires' (I, preliminaries; p. 96). Right at the beginning of his
career he already guesses that it will end unhappily because he
failed to attend mass one Sunday (I, i, 6; p. 182): subsequently he
does not abandon his pious observances even in his most extreme
periods of degradation;[15] and at the end of his long journey, roped
together with the other prisoners, the galley slave reflects 'If we
have all this to suffer here, if this chain is such a torture... what
must those who are condemned to eternal punishment feel?' (II,
iii, 8; p. 876). Or conversely, during his virtuous periods, the voice
of evil makes itself heard: 'I was still trapped up to my neck in the
quagmire of vices. Because even though I was not practising
them, I never lost sight of them' (II, ii, 2; pp. 599–600). This bitter
inner conflict is the constant feature of his life before the conversion. The beginning of each main phase of his life is marked by the
necessity of making a painful decision; but the really serious
problem is that the dilemma faces him afresh at every moment:
Guzmán is responsible for himself and continually has choices to
make;[16] and since reason and faith pull him in one direction and
will and instinct in another, he keeps fluctuating from one
extreme to the other, in the grip of a constant inner turmoil.

Alemán devotes his greatest gifts as a novelist (in the most
traditional sense of the word) to this portrait of a divided soul.
One cannot help recalling the figure of Guzmanillo in Rome, as a
member of the beggars' guild. While posing as a false cripple, the
boy is aware that every time he is given alms it is so much money
stolen from the genuinely poor, and that this puts him under an

obligation to pay it back; and thus he lives in a permanent state of unease: 'On the one hand I was happy when they gave me something; on the other, I trembled inwardly when I took stock of my life..., knowing for certain that I was on the way to damnation' (I, iii, 6; p. 395). It is worth recalling briefly one further particularly successful scene. Guzmán, already on the downward path which leads to the galleys, has contrived a trick to win the confidence of a certain friar and make him an innocent accomplice to his own evil plans: it involves giving him a purse full of money that he says he found (he has already arranged for someone to claim it), so that the friar will announce it during his sermon on Sunday. Such a streak of honesty, in so apparently needy a person as Guzmán, moves the good friar and makes him burst into a flood of praises. But though each word of praise takes the *pícaro* one step nearer his goal, at the same time it cuts him to the heart: 'While he was saying this to me he was driving the iron into my soul, because when I considered his saintliness and simplicity as against my malice and knavery – for I was trying by these means to make him an instrument for my own theft – I burst into tears' (II, iii, 6; p. 857). It is at moments such as this that Guzmán's spiritual dialectic is crystallized with particular clarity; but an entire lifetime spent fluctuating between good and evil bears out the fact that this type of struggle constitutes the most characteristic feature of his personality.[17]

This inner conflict, either in itself or in its consequences, is undoubtedly the main theme of the story. For on the one hand it is so frequently reiterated as to become the touchstone and common denominator of every phase of Guzmán's biography: and on the other, it delimits the work and determines its structure: it advances the action by creating the conflict, and completes the action by resolving it.

Moreover, it so happens that this disjunction within the pro-tagonist is appropriately reflected in the style. We have only to focus on the monologues of Guzmán the actor and we will soon discover that, paradoxically, they often turn out to be dialogues. '"God help me!", I began to think to myself, "for this concerns me too, and I am somebody! Account is being taken of me! What light can I give to others – how can there even be any light in so vile and abject a person and way of life?" "Yes, my friend," I answered myself, "it concerns you and he is speaking to you, for you too are a member of this mystical body..." ' (' "¡Válgame Dios!– me puse a pensar –, que aún a mí me toca, y yo soy alguien: ¡cuenta se hace de mí! ¿Pues qué luz puedo dar o cómo la puede haber en hombre y en oficio tan escuro y bajo?" "Sí, amigo – me respondía –, a ti te toca y contigo habla, que también eres miembro deste cuerpo místico..." ', I, ii, 3; pp. 267–8). Alone, isolated on the fringes of society, friendless (despite wanting friends 'desperately'; II, ii, 1, p. 582), Guzmanillo carries on a dialogue with the other *I* of his divided self: he questions and – when he can – he answers, advises, accuses, and encourages.

The use of the second person, whether explicit or disguised in the form of a rhetorical or allegorical debate, had a venerable tradition in spiritual prose and had long been present in the preaching and moral literature of the period; in our novel and in the speeches of Guzmán the author, it frequently stands for Guzmán the character or for the reader (and sometimes both),[18] suggesting the tension between ethical imperatives and disorderly conduct, between sinful youth and virtuous maturity. In Guzmanillo's reflections, the most apposite – though not the only – use of the second person (*tú*) is as an economical means of giving concrete expression to a divided consciousness, tormented by the necessity of choosing between the voice of instinct and the motions of grace. Accordingly, the critical moment of the conversion is presented in the second person: 'I said to myself one night: "Guzmán, can't you [*tú*] see that you're on the summit of the mountain of miseries to which your wicked sensuality has brought you? You are now at the top, and you can either leap off into the abyss of hell, or just by raising your arm, you can easily reach heaven..." ' (II, ii, 8; p. 889). Thus, merely by the use of the second-person form, the most decisive moment in the novel emerges as a natural solution to the debate which has been tormenting the protagonist: it is the triumph of one half of his soul over the other.

Some will feel that precisely this internal conflict within Guzmán in itself makes it unconvincing that he should be converted to the ways of virtue (rather than becoming hardened to his

evil), let alone definitively converted. Let us avoid useless psychological speculations (in which we could find confirmation of the
most widely differing prejudices);[19] what really does need to be
pointed out is that Mateo Alemán would not have seen this as a
problem, but rather as an answer, and one which, among a great
many other things, he aimed to reveal to us and to demonstrate for
us in his book: for Alemán, Guzmanillo's conflict would have been
both a presage and a proof of his final salvation.

The course of his experiences – stumbling, falling and repent-
ing – is quite clearly designed to teach us the lesson of free will:
man is his own master and chooses his destiny, there is no such
thing as '*this must be so* or *it is right that this should be so*, you make it be
so and make it right that it should' (i, iii, 10; p. 437). This is one of
the book's unambiguous theses.[20] Now as a thesis, and as a fact of
experience, human freedom leaves the outcome open: Guzmán
could incline towards good or towards evil, persevere or give up.
As far as contemporary thought was concerned, however, the
conflict within the sinner – the corollary of his freedom – was at
the same time quite a strong hint of a happy ending: a sign, in fact,
that this dilemma would be resolved with the triumph of good and
perseverance.

This idea, which belongs in the sphere of pastoral practice
rather than dogma, was formulated with great clarity by Fray
Pedro Malón de Chaide; and it is worth quoting the passage in full
– in preference to other similar ones – not only because it is so
specific, but also because it comes from an Augustinian friar, and
can thus be legitimately taken to represent the *opinio communis* of
an order for whose patron and members Alemán seems to have
felt a singular affection.[21] Fray Pedro comments on the unfath-
omable nature of Divine Providence, using the conversion of
Mary Magdalen as a starting point, and pausing at length to
include some observations that quickly make the reader of the
Guzmán feel he is in a familiar environment:

You will find some sinners who, even though they are sinners, have
something indescribable about them even in the midst of their evil lives,
a hint and an appearance of being predestined to glory and of being the
children of God, a respect for virtue, an abhorrence of vice, a sense of fear
even as they sin and a constant state of terror, a 'this life is not for me, I

was not born for this'; in short, they do not seem to be addicted to
sinning. You will see other sinners so set in their ways and so unconcerned at their sin that it seems natural to them: people who give free
rein to their sin, so inured to vice that, instead of waiting for vices to
come to them, they go out and seek them ... Well now, this is what
Eliphaz means [Job 15. 16]: that there are some sinners who devour the
very sins they commit: that is, they take heed of them and brood on the
evil they do and take heed of it. These are the ones of whom we say that
the fact that they must be of the elect is written on their faces. But there
are others who sin without the slightest revulsion, swallowing their sins
without chewing, with the greatest of ease, so much so that they already
seem to be showing signs of their own perdition.[22]

Guzmanillo obviously belongs to the first category, those who are
conscious sinners and are even tormented by their disgust and
fear; he falls into the ranks of those who 'are left with a feeling of
annoyance and bitterness towards [sin] and with a certain naus-
eous revulsion towards vice, whose anger and shame is directed
towards themselves';[23] and for this very reason the fact that he
must be 'of the elect' is 'written on his face'.

We began by identifying a constant feature of the protagonist:
his bitter inner conflict. In an excessively cursory but I trust still
intelligible manner, we have followed this through on three
distinct planes: firstly as one element in the definition of an
individual personality, secondly in one of its linguistic formu-
lations, and thirdly as a vehicle for a particular doctrine. By
showing that they are related, and that each is directed towards
the same target, we hinted that these three planes converge on the
decisive moment of the conversion. It is now time to point out, in
conclusion, that they also come together in just the same way to
explain – from within, through the fiction itself – the book's very
existence and nature. On the human level, Guzmán's inner
conflict is the product of a vigilant conscience, of his turning in on
himself in order to call himself to account; accordingly, the
writing of the autobiography turns out to be an act of introspection. On the stylistic level, the second person, which reflects
Guzmanillo's dual nature, is used again later by Guzmán the
author to designate Guzmán the actor: the dialogue is now
conducted across a gap in time, and the convert reflects on the
fortunes of the *pícaro* (although now without his former unease),

just as one of the *pícaro*'s selves previously reflected on the other. On the doctrinal level, this inner conflict in the character fore-shadows his final repentance, and thereby helps us to understand the more readily that the sermons with which the work is pep-pered come from a Guzmán who has solved his dilemma by inclining towards good,[24] and that by the same token, as a proof of his contrition and out of a desire to serve as an example, he does not hesitate to portray himself as evil – even exaggerating his faults like a new St Augustine in some new *Confessions* – and to heap misfortune, disrespect and ridicule on himself.

The Watchtower of Life

Let us recall *Lazarillo de Tormes*: there, the structure of the story was determined by the way in which the principal narrative units converge towards 'the case' of the final chapter. Similarly, in *Guzmán de Alfarache*, the protagonist's various adventures (which can be reduced in every case to the more or less long-lasting predominance of one of the two violently conflicting tendencies within him) are seen to be directed towards the final conversion.

But the conversion, of course, meant the complete espousal of a dogma and demanded the adoption of a single point of view, a faith which offered universal solutions. This dogma and this point of view obviously existed before Guzmanillo; but he, though always aware of their demands, only manages to attain them in their entirety as a conclusion and corollary of his whole life. They are therefore *a priori* ideas demonstrated *a posteriori* by the *pícaro*'s experience. Carlos Blanco Aguinaga, in a masterly essay,[25] has presented this explanation and I will not dwell on it here except to illustrate it by briefly citing one very simple example.

The Council of Trent had taught that faith without works is not enough to justify man and that God's grace will unfailingly come to the aid of anyone who combines the two. Guzmán knows this; and when, for example, he leaves Rome 'determined to be an honourable man' (ii, ii, 2; p. 598), but not very willing to face up to the difficult consequences of his aim, 'I went along', he says, 'struggling with myself'; and sure enough, he soon reverts to evil ways. By contrast, when he adds good works to his intention to reform, he immediately has something with which 'to buy grace': 'Put all those trials, your sufferings and your efforts, ... into God's account. ... Because when you give it all to Him, He will combine your wealth with His own, and as He makes it all infinitely valuable, you will enjoy eternal life' (II, iii, 8; p. 890). In this way, Guzmán's experience has come to confirm Tridentine dogma. The fictitious author has absorbed this dogma into his consciousness point by point; it is no longer a belief but rather an empirical certainty incorporated into an individual worldview. By the same token, when writing his autobiography, Guzmán can progressively expound this truth that has dominated the course of his life, in a series of apposite discourses.[26] This article of faith is both the first premiss in the syllogism of his existence and the final conclusion of his experience.

Thus the doctrine presented to us in an explicitly developed form both emerges from the story, and informs it, in the sense that it constitutes Guzmán's point of view. The 'opinions', the didacticism in its purest form, are woven into the 'life', the narration, in various ways.[27] There are, however, two essential types of discourse, which reflect the characteristically dual nature of these fluctuations of viewpoint. On the one hand, there are sermons presented as theoretical, generalizing commentaries on specific incidents or facts: sermons which reconstruct the path which has led Guzmán to his dogmatic high point as a 'perfect man',[28] and put the lived experience of the past into the perspective and the context of the present in which he is writing, absorbing this experience in so far as it points towards the final conversion. On the other hand, there are a number of *moralités* introduced as theoretical premises for an event or piece of information, so that a conceptual structure is projected onto the character's concrete experiences.[29] Abstract doctrine is embodied in the individual or crystallized in the particular situation, and there is nothing surprising in this: if the fortunes of Guzmán the actor tended to account for the nature of Guzmán the author, and showed us the gradual acquisition of a point of view, then everything could flow from this point of view, proceeding 'from the definition to the thing defined' (I, i, I; p. 105), from the painfully acquired doctrine to the life that confirmed it. In this way, whether the narrative precedes the discourse or the discourse precedes the narrative, each nucleus of the novel draws together the whole course of the protagonist's career, connects the actor and the author – each in all his complexity, reminds us of the general framework of the novel and reinforces the motivation underlying the plot.[30]

The autobiographical form of *Guzmán de Alfarache* was probably adopted in response to several different stimuli. The example of St Augustine's *Confessions* (and 'confession', as we know, is one of the names the narrator gives his book) predisposed the reader to accept an autobiography 'whose purpose is to edify the reader by revealing the author's own errors',[31] while at the same time commenting on these errors and interpreting them as stages in the process of a conversion. *Lazarillo de Tormes* had sanctioned the use of the fictitious memoirs of a vagabond as a pretext for a novel and shown how to structure them in a 'closed narrative',[32] directing them toward a specific conclusion ('the case', the conversion), which in turn was able to explain the origin and the organization of the story. On another level, one must remember that in 1593, as a visiting judge at the mines of Almadén, Mateo Alemán spent almost two months listening to and taking down autobiographical depositions from men condemned to hard labour (among them, a friar and a poet) who were serving their sentences there, thanks to a decree of Philip II that allowed them to exchange the oars of a galley slave for mining equipment.[33]

All these factors, and doubtless others as well, must have turned Alemán's attention towards autobiography. But he was also led to adopt it by the dual purpose – literary and exemplary – of the work he was planning. For the fact is that if the third person had been used, the explicit doctrine would have seemed too artificially superimposed on the story and would therefore have weakened it, militating against Guzmán's verisimilitude and autonomy: by distancing him at every stage from the real author, it would have sharpened the impression that the protagonist was a figurehead, a mere insubstantial puppet used as a vehicle for someone else's theses. But in the first-person form, the explicit doctrine was inseparably integrated into the fiction (we have already seen some of the skilful means by which this is done), creating the illusion that it arises naturally out of actions and states of mind, confirming the consistency of Guzmán – from character to writer – and being itself confirmed in his experiences. Thus autobiographical form enables the creation of a character and the presentation of a series of didactic messages – literature and pedagogy – to reinforce one another.

And Mateo Alemán handles this form so shrewdly that even the specific constraints of the first person acquire artistic value. He is extremely careful, for example, to maintain the illusion of authenticity: Guzmán always records his source of information for those scenes in which he is not present, he distinguishes between what he has witnessed and what he suspects, enters numerous caveats, and so on.[34] *Sub specie aeternitatis*, we may quite reasonably regret the exclusion of those beautifully narrated pages (as they would undoubtedly have been, coming from Alemán) that the autobiographical presentation has denied us. But we are handsomely compensated for them, in that the necessity of establishing the self as the measure of all things forces the narrator to explore it more profoundly, to give it greater consistency, to shape it more fully. One example will suffice. Guzmán, now rich after gaining his revenge, returns to Genoa, leaving behind him some relatives who are bound to discover very soon that they have been tricked. Obviously the author is not in a position to portray what must have happened in Italy while the rogue was sailing toward Spain; but on the other hand he does now have an opportunity to develop his portrait of the protagonist more subtly, by following the flight of his imagination:

I had only one wish during the whole journey, which was to know what the innkeeper thought when I failed to return to the inn that first day, and on the second, seeing I was nowhere to be found, I expect they must have wept for me. What cold shivers I must have given them! How many blankets they must have thrown on themselves, and yet given none to the hospital!* How diligently they must have searched for me! What guesses they must have made about where I could be, whether I had been killed and robbed of some of my winnings, or whether I had been wounded!...

Sólo un deseo llevé todo el camino, que fue de saber, cuando aquel primero día no volviese a la posada, qué pensaría el huésped: y al segundo, cuando no me hallasen, paréceme que llorarían todos por mí.

* [*Translator's note*. There is an untranslatable pun here: *echar mantas* means (literally) 'to throw blankets' and also 'to curse'.]

¡Cuántos escalofríos les daría! ¡Qué de mantas echarían, y ninguna en el hospital! ¡Qué diligencias harían en buscarme! ¡Qué de juicios echarían sobre adónde podría estar, si me habrían muerto por quitarme alguna ganancia o si me habrían herido!... (ii, ii, 8; p. 707)

The passage in question (of which this is only a part) serves us as a succinct illustration of an essential feature of the book: one of Mateo Alemán's prime concerns is to express in novelistic form the consciousness – past and present – of the protean Alfarache, and he revels in the minutely detailed analysis of subjectivity. In the passage quoted above the emphasis is obviously on recording Guzmán's imagination at work (and his is a nature with a propensity towards flights of fantasy, speculations and complications, if ever there was one), on showing us not only the results, but also the precise development of a mental process. Guzmán, as actor and as author, thinks or contemplates and is aware of himself thinking or contemplating: on every level, point of view interests him at least as much as what is actually viewed.

This explains why the action is often diluted in emotions (and also, on the other hand, in values) and why the reader has to reconstruct it starting from Guzmán's own consciousness. Except for their common use of the first person, in some cases, this technique is diametrically opposed to that of the *nouveau roman*. The perfect 'objective novelist' confines the narrator to the role of an impassive camera, and moreover, in the parody by Salvador Clotas, 'instead of writing "John is nervous"..., he will write "John smokes a cigarette, John stubs out the cigarette, John smokes another cigarette"'.[35] Whereas Guzmán prefers to show us himself being nervous and merely hint at the causes of this nervousness, noting, for instance, that the third day after his escape 'almost finished me off, everything got on top of me at once' and concentrating not on the 'hardships' that he suffered, but rather on the emotions and ideas that these suggested to him (i, ii, 1; pp. 247–50).

It also explains why evocation is more prevalent than description in the strict sense of the word, and why Guzmán constantly resorts to a kind of interior monologue *avant la lettre*,[36] reflecting mental processes with remarkable aesthetic fidelity. Thus when he enters the school of love, at the expense of being torn away from the lecture theatres of Alcalá:

'How could this have been anything but a bad night for me? What long hours, what little sleep, what turbulent thoughts, what overwhelming struggle, what turmoil of conflicting cares, what storm has blown up in the haven of my greatest prosperity?', I said. 'How can such a tempest have shattered my secure tranquillity, without me even being aware it was coming, or how to find a solution? I am utterly lost. There is no certain prospect of relief in my distress...' (II, iii, 4; p. 820)

The passage quoted at length a little earlier disintegrated in a string of exclamations; this one builds up a series of questions. In both cases the tone is created by the affective quality of the prose. Or again, consider the passage devoted to relating and commenting on Guzmán's reactions to a card game:

They [the players] were not in the least upset, yet I was, for no earthly reason apart from looking at his cards, when he [the cardplayer whose cards Guzmán saw] either failed to win or lost outright. Oh what a strange nature we have, not only myself but everyone in general! For although these people were not known to me, not a single one of them, and I had never seen them before, for that was the first time... and I had never had any dealings with them, I felt glad when the fellow I wanted to win did so. What a useless sin mine was! How stupid and pointless to wish that the others should lose so that he might win! As if those winnings were mine, as if they had taken them from me or were going to give them to me! How foolish we are to put another man's burdens on our own shoulders...! Some woman stands looking out of her window, some man at his door, spying on their neighbour's house to see who came out before dawn or who went in at midnight, what they brought in or what they took out ... Brother, sister, get away from there! May God help all of us, whatever we do or leave undone. For it may be that you are the sinner, and not she. What do her life or death, her comings or goings, have to do with you? What do you gain, what advantage do you get, from spending such a miserable night? What honour do you get out of her dishonour? What pleasure do you derive from all this?... (II, ii, 3; pp. 619–20)

And so on.

We could cite a great many similar passages,[37] all of them animated by a feeling that is sometimes woven into complex periods, which explore every nuance of it and are finally summed up in an incisive phrase, and is sometimes fragmented into abrupt outbursts of irritation, anxious questions or fluent, spontaneous expressions of sarcasm. But for the moment it is enough to point out that this affective intensity that pervades the style of the *Guzmán*, besides defining the fictitious author (and the real one, of course; for our present purposes this is merely a happy coincidence), is a genuine symptom of the principle which determines the whole structure of the work: the presentation of every element in it in terms of an essentially coherent self. Thus Guzmán's highly charged prose is one of the factors which enable us to recognize the presence of a substantial degree of psychological realism in the novel.

Of course, the reasons for this emotional stance on the narrator's part vary considerably, but it seems clear that it arises particularly often from a contrast between men and situations on the one hand, and religious values on the other. The last passage quoted above strikes me as highly characteristic: Guzmán the actor becomes emotionally involved in a scene (as he watched the cardplayers, he says, 'I was beside myself', p. 619); Guzmán the author takes note of the evidence, generalizes it, and compares it with the demands of Christian morality, in an outburst of heated invective which prolongs the rogue's passion from a different perspective.

This fact, which is highly significant in novelistic terms, interests me at this stage only as a piece of historical evidence: that is to say I think the fact that *Guzmán* is so much concerned with examining the psyche is inseparable from its substantial religious element. Faith, by definition, is an inner phenomenon. And presenting a religious dilemma as the central theme – a dilemma resolved in the conversion – necessarily involved a profound exploration of the character's soul. Religious life and literature favoured the enterprise: not for nothing were spiritual meditation and the 'examination of conscience' such common practices,[38] and not for nothing did Christianity have at its disposal both a well-established typology with which to interpret mental states,[39] and an immensely rich tradition (largely following St Augustine) of devotional prose which was exceptionally well versed in the expression of the very finest nuances of emotion and intellect.[40] But following on from this background, so intimate an exploration of Guzmán's religious sensibility led the author to a profound investigation of the other aspects of his innermost soul, thus rounding off the complete portrait of the character.

But there is more to it than that. The considerable religious significance of the central fictional and doctrinal elements goes a long way towards explaining one of the most original aspects of the work in the context of contemporary literature: the completely serious presentation of Guzmán, and the fact that he is endowed with a full and unmistakable individuality, instead of being confined to the purely contemptible role to which the rustic type was normally limited in the literature of the period.[41] According to the poetics of the time (and not even Shakespeare violated this rule), a lowly character was by definition a comic character. But Alemán gave his character a tragic dimension, rescuing him from the entirely simple role he would normally have been assigned, and investing him with the complexity of real life. Alemán does not seem to have felt very much sympathy for 'those of obscure lineage, lowly birth and despicable thoughts' (I, dedication; p. 89). But to focus on Alfarache specifically as a *homo religiosus* meant neither more nor less than taking him to be 'equal with everyone else in essence, even though not in rank' (I, ii, 3; p. 268), and precluded treating him as a stereotyped member of his social class. Having created him in order to show (among other things) that there is no such thing as '*this must be so* or *it is right that this should be so*' (I, iii, 10; p. 437), but rather that all men are endowed with free will,[42] Alemán was obliged to give his character real autonomy, quite outside the prevailing literary conventions. Thus, didactic purposes and religious dogma did not turn the protagonist into a cardboard figure, as characters usually are in *romans à thèse*; on the contrary, they led the author to endow him with a fully-rounded personality, and, accordingly, prompted him to conceive Guzmán's character from within. This is also what makes the autobiographical form so profoundly appropriate.

The portrait of Guzmán, then, is complete and fully rounded. But is it achieved at the expense of secondary characters? It is indeed. With very few exceptions, these subsidiary characters are sketched in with a single stroke of the pen, and are limited to a bare embodiment of the vice that is to be castigated or the virtue that is offered as a model (the latter case being confined to clerics). By comparison with the rich individuality of Guzmán, they strike us as one-dimensional. Of course, this sort of simplification depends on an *a priori* assumption (man's deep-seated evil, an effect of original sin,[43] on the one hand, and the perfection of the religious life on the other), and for modern tastes, the artistic stature of the novel is thereby diminished. But we should not overlook the fact that this procedure is beautifully integrated into the essentially unified plot structure of the novel (and far from seriously weakening it, in my opinion, it is concealed and supported within it). We noted above that Guzmán confines himself to reporting what he sees, hears, feels or thinks, in such a way that the illusion of reality is completely flawless. But we must now add that this admirable handling of the autobiographical form is fully consistent with the fact that secondary characters are reduced to a single feature – namely, that feature of them which affects the protagonist. Guzmán perceives them in passing, superficially, without capturing their inner selves, which he can only reconstruct by analogy with himself.[44] Neither as actor nor as author can he be impartial: men are either categorized according to one of the two extremes of his life before the conversion, or they are presented in the light of his firm and universal beliefs as a convert and judged as strictly and passionately as he judges himself. In the novel, as characters, they have to be filtered through Guzmán's consciousness, and adapted to fit its dimensions.

However we approach the problem, we always end up at the same point. In our novel, the realities which are reflected, and the ways in which they are reflected, are meaningless unless they are seen in relation to Guzmán, unless we realize that they are *things which happen to* Guzmán. Thus the essence of the novel is not so much a question of showing us things as of presenting Guzmán to us in the act of perceiving them and absorbing them into his consciousness. Alemán indicated this in his very title: *The Life of Guzmán de Alfarache, Watchtower of Human Life*. By definition the work set out to show us 'human life' from a particular point of view, from a 'watchtower' explicitly recognized as such.[45] The successful accomplishment of this object – organizing all the component parts in terms of a point of view, and explaining the latter by the former – is where Mateo Alemán's literary achievement lies: it is not my object here to explore how far this point of view may also be a point of weakness, a cross-current in the history of the modern novel.[46]

The picaresque novel and the point of view

– And who are you? – said he.
– Don't puzzle me ...

Tristram Shandy

The novel slipped through Spain's fingers.

José F. Montesinos

The popularity of the Lazarillo

Lazarillo de Tormes was a popular book in the time of Philip II.[1] However, its success in the sixteenth century can hardly be measured by the number of editions published in the Peninsula and known to us today: erudite bibliographers have only just managed to register a bare half-dozen printings before 1599.[2] This total is by no means negligible, but it is still far from overwhelming. In any case, I think we should use it as an indication, and not as a conclusion. For the fact is that because of its irreverent allusions and its faint air of scepticism the novel was placed on the *Catalogue of Prohibited Books* (1559) of the Inquisitor Fernando de Valdés. And to anyone familiar with the zeal with which the Holy Office characteristically strove to eliminate the slightest trace of proscribed works, it will come as no surprise that the only surviving evidence from the decisive years of its rapid rise to fame, the years immediately following its first appearance (1552 or 1553?), consists of two editions (both, naturally, preserved in foreign libraries, and in single copies).

However, the fact that the work was prohibited did not mean that it was consigned to oblivion: it circulated in manuscript,[3] and doubtless some people managed to smuggle in a few copies of some foreign edition. In fact the demand must have been so persistent that in 1573, with a new Inquisitor and a more flexible approach to censorship, the Royal Council authorized the reprinting of the *Lazarillo*, with the fourth and fifth chapters excised, as well as several passages of blatant irreverence and excessively direct criticism. Juan López de Velasco, who was responsible for the expurgation, justified it by recalling that the book 'was always very well received by everyone; and for this reason, even though it was prohibited in these realms, it was read [i.e. here, in Spain] and regularly printed outside them'.[4] But obviously those 'outside them' had absolutely no need of a reprint, let alone an expurgated version. It was the Spanish public that wanted to be able to enjoy the fortunes and misfortunes of Lázaro; and the best policy, in view of the danger that they might get hold of a complete text, was to make it available to them in a mutilated form (Spaniards of my generation will recognize the procedure).

But let us not get sidetracked here in interpretations of the bibliographical evidence, or speculations as to whether or not the little novel was disseminated in fragile, neglected *pliegos sueltos* (broadsheets). What is certain is that the *Lazarillo* was to make a deep impression on the popular consciousness, so deep that by 1587 it had already been immortalized to the extent of having given rise to popular proverbs.[5] If we turn from the people at large to the intellectual aristocracy, we find that as early as 1563 the great Zurita considered the book to be as widely familiar as common *hablillas* (popular folk tales),[6] and a few years later we catch Pedro Simón Abril illustrating a law of physics with an episode from the town crier's youthful adventures: 'Lázaro de Tormes', he writes, 'knew how to take advantage [of this law] in order to sip the poor blind man's wine, which I believe he must have learned by having been born and reared in Salamanca, a place so full of natural intelligence and copious learning.'[7] Around 1589, an encyclopedic moralist, Fray Juan de Pineda, delighted in repeatedly citing episodes and characters from the work (the blow on the head against the stone bull, the priest feasting at other people's expense, the 'gloomy house', the squire ...), referring to them with the brevity and familiarity of one who knew that even the smallest details of content and style were well known to everyone.[8]

Creative literature welcomed Lazarillo with open arms. Sebastián de Horozco, for instance, put him on the stage;[9] and in 1593 Luis de Góngora, no less, while recovering from a sickness and feeling love-sick, recalled him in a splendid sonnet, which

could not be understood without a precise knowledge of the
novel:

> Muerto me lloró el Tormes en su orilla,
> en un parasismal sueño profundo,
> en cuanto don Apolo el rubicundo
> tres veces sus caballos desensilla.
>   Fue mi resurrección la maravilla
> que de Lázaro fue la vuelta al mundo,
> de suerte que ya soy otro segundo
> Lazarillo de Tormes en Castilla.
>   Entré a servir a un ciego, que me envía;
> sin alma vivo, y en dulce fuego
> que ceniza hará la vida mía.
>   ¡Oh qué dichoso que sería yo luego,
> si a Lazarillo le imitase un día
> en la venganza que tomó del ciego![10]

> The River Tormes wept for me as I lay dead on its
>   banks,
> In a deep sleep of paralysis,
> While red-haired Lord Apollo
> Thrice unsaddles his horses.
>   My resurrection was the same miracle
> As Lazarus's return to the world,
> So that I am now a second
> Lazarillo de Tormes in Castille.
>   I entered the service of one blind, who leads me;
> I live without a soul, and in a sweet fire
> Which will turn my life to ashes.
>   Oh how happy I would be at once
> Were I to imitate Lazarillo one day
> In the revenge he took on the blind man!

The book and its protagonist did not always fare so well: one of the
anonymous continuations (Antwerp, 1555) had turned Lázaro
into a mere puppet and had retrospectively obliterated the design
of the work by incorporating it into the fantastic genre of the story
of 'transformations';[11] and if Shakespeare's Benedick recalled 'the
boy that stole [the blind man's] meate' directly from our novel
(and not from the *Mery Tales* of 1567),[12] Luis de Pinedo had
stupidly reduced it to a collection of funny stories:[13] precisely the
model that the *Lazarillo* was attempting to transcend. On the
other hand, Juan de Timoneda, before 1599, highlighted one
characteristic of the protagonist (his sharp-wittedness) and one

element of the work's construction (the series of masters) that were to be distinguishing features of the whole of the picaresque; in the *Menechmos*, in fact, Averróiz the doctor declares that his servant 'is the sharpest lad in the world and a true brother of Lazarillo de Tormes, the one who had three hundred and fifty masters'.[14] Whatever the particular case, it is surprising how vivid and lasting an impression even the most fleeting images from the *Lazarillo* made on the literary consciousness of the time. Father Buendía, before 1577, recalls the squire and the vain ostentation with which he picks his teeth, and Góngora, between 1581 and 1593, uses and abuses the motif of 'the honourable toothpick', closely following our novel; not much later, the *Farsa del triunfo del Sacramento* (The Triumph of the Sacrament) recollects the image of the 'gloomy, sad house ... where no one eats', and a certain *Entreacto* invents a new episode in Lazarillo's adventures; around 1568, Eugenio de Salazar brilliantly portrays the ease with which a servant becomes inured to dreadful village food 'with far fewer scruples than Lazarillo de Tormes's master, because he [the squire] at least asked whether the crumbs came from bread kneaded with clean hands'.[15] And so on.

All that was lacking was someone capable of perceiving that the *Lazarillo* constituted a unique literary entity, one which it was not appropriate to incorporate into other types of fiction but which, on the contrary, invited others to imitate it as a *commencement absolu*.[16] Timoneda, who was always willing to take advantage of material from other writers, must have had some inkling of this when he likened the boy in the *Menechmos* to the protagonist of our novel, and above all, when in his short comic play the *Paso de dos ciegos y un mozo* (Two Blind Men and a Boy) he introduced Palillos, in search of a new master, and had him recount in an exculpatory tone the experiences he had while serving a blind man who was starving him to death. Timoneda was not the man to grasp how to take full advantage of the copious possibilities that the thematic conception and the autobiographical form of the *Lazarillo* offered to a skilful writer. But Palillos, that paltry individual of lowly estate who presumes to narrate in the first person a story that aims to compete with that of Lázaro de Tormes, is perhaps the earliest manifestation of an archetype that puts us at the very threshold of a new genre: the picaresque novel.

From literature to life

The reason we nowadays speak of a given novel as *picaresque*[17] is that when the first part of *The Life of Guzmán de Alfarache, Watchtower of Human Life* was published, its readers, extracting one common denominator (out of several possible ones) from the various stages of the protagonist's career, and reducing the title to a kind of nickname, 'took to calling it *Pícaro*' ('dieron en llamarle *Pícaro*', II, i, 6; p. 546).[18] But to characterize the picaresque novel exclusively by reference to the real-life type of the *pícaro* or to the archetype of everyday 'picaresque' life is a futile exercise: what may fruitfully be attempted, however, is to approach this task on the basis of the *character*, the *literary creation* which is the *Pícaro*.

And while doing so, we should not forget a perceptive remark made by Umberto Eco: 'We know Julien Sorel better than our own father. Because many moral traits of the latter, many unexpressed thoughts, undivulged feelings, well-kept secrets, memories and incidents from his childhood will always remain unknown to us ... whereas we know everything about Julien Sorel that we have any *interest* in knowing. And this is the important thing: our father is part of life, and in life – in history, as Aristotle would say – so many things happen one after another that it is impossible for us to piece together the complex pattern of their sequence. Julien Sorel, by contrast, is a product of imagination and art, and art selects and composes only *what counts* as regards the final goal of an action and its organic, convincing development.'[19] Exactly. The real-life *pícaro* dissolves into a thousand unassimilable facets; the novelistic *pícaro* is distinguished precisely by order and sequence (sometimes organic, sometimes ossified, but always present).

In the first place, the word *pícaro* (whose etymology is problematic)[20] seems to have gained wide currency in the last third of the sixteenth century as denoting an individual – generally a child or a young boy – who was 'contemptible and of lowly condition, with wretched clothes and the appearance of a man of little honour' (as Fray Diego de Guadix puts it).[21] In fact, the 'wretched clothes', the rags and the grime are logical extensions of the 'little honour'. The *pícaro* does not have a status defined by rights and obligations, such as the need to 'mantener honra' ('maintain one's honour'). On the contrary, in a prevailing situation of minimal social mobility, he is distinguished by a lack of ties: nothing binds him for long to a particular place, master or task.

His parents may have been vagrants,[22] or he may have escaped from the strict tutelage of a father or master; he has grown up in the streets and has learned to get on in life by the sweat of other men's brows, by dint of cunning ruses and knavish tricks. In order to keep himself going and to evade the law against vagrants and delinquents, he occasionally looks for a job, something that does not require him to work too hard or tie him down too per-manently. And so around 1550, he is sometimes to be found in the kitchens of great houses (or even of the palace), employed as a casual scullion or kitchen boy, his only pay, of course, being his 'keep'.[23] Half a century later, round about 1600, the favourite activity of the *pícaro* (to the extent that more than once the term is used to refer exclusively to this occupation) is that of the *espor-tillero*, or *ganapán* (porter, errand boy or messenger, as we would say), standing around in markets and commercial districts with a little basket and a rope halter, ready to carry packages or to do odd jobs for a few coppers.[24] This is the sort of thing an errand boy's job involves; as for their free time, a contemporary tells us, 'whenever they are not working, they are playing cards together, and then they move on to cheap bars and taverns, accompanied day and night by wanton women [*pícaras perdidas*]'.[25] To sum up in a few words (written in 1585), 'they live free and easy ... just as they please',[26] savouring the 'sweets of the picaresque life' (*almíbar picaresco*; this term comes from Guzmán himself, 1, ii, 2; p. 261). Sebastián de Covarrubias, the greatest lexicographer of the period, is thinking of just such porters when he observes that, though *pícaros* are not '[slaves or servants] of anyone in particular, they serve the commonwealth in general, for the benefit of anyone who wants to hire them and give them menial jobs to do'.[27]

The *pícaro*'s temporary jobs are menial indeed, and they often verge on delinquency when they are not completely involved in it. In the court, together with the 'sound masonry', Eugenio de Salazar already found an enormous 'heap of rubble ... consisting of rogues, profligates, villains, murderers, thieves, cloak snatch-

ers, cardsharpers, cheats, imposters, swindlers, flatterers, huck-
sters, forgers, ruffians, '*pícaros*', *vagabonds and other evildoers*'.[28]
Exceptionally, the *pícaro* can be 'virtuous, clean, well bred and of
more than average prudence', like Carriazo in Cervantes's *La
ilustre fregona* (The Illustrious Kitchen Maid); but 'among those
called *pícaros*', in the view of so perceptive a witness as Cervantes
himself, one finds as a rule 'dirty, fat, flashy kitchen boys; false
paupers, sham cripples, cutpurses in Zocodover [in Toledo] and
the Plaza Mayor in Madrid, blind beggars who can see perfectly
well, errand boys from Seville, underworld hangers-on ... an
innumerable rabble...'.[29]

The fauna was certainly varied, and each specimen was essentially changeable. This is why assessments of the *pícaro* – as of the
street urchin (*golfo*) in Madrid around 1900,[30] to cite a well-known
parallel – fluctuated between the most diverse possibilities. Thus
at times the *pícaro* came to epitomize everything pernicious and
contemptible; at other times he was idealized as a mirror for
philosophers, a remote descendant of Diogenes; often he became
the very incarnation of ingenuity and shrewdness. There is
nothing surprising in this. The abundant 'literature of roguery'
bears out the fact that from recognizing evil skills to admiring
them as art forms has never been more than a short step.
Moreover, 'outsiders' – whether one calls them goliards,
bohemians or hippies – have always enjoyed a certain sentimental
prestige. In the case we are examining, it is no accident – as
Marcel Bataillon has explained – that the success of the picaresque occurred in a period of the headlong pursuit of honour and
the apogee of social conventions:[31] the figure of the *pícaro*, free from
all social constraints, doubtless expressed aspirations which
Habsburg Spain, haunted by the spectre of genealogies and by the
obligation of keeping up honourable appearances, dared not
confess unless it disguised them with ironies and jokes, and
dressed them up in paradoxes.

The picture I have presented here is deficient, but it should be
adequate in this context. For our present purposes, it should make
it clear why Guzmán de Alfarache called himself a *pícaro* during
his days as an errand boy and false pauper – when he is entirely
his own master – and why he explicitly rejects the term when he

settles down to serve a master:[32] because he uses it as a substantive rather than an adjective, that is, in order to designate himself as a member of a social and (to some extent) professional class, rather than to connote a set of qualities and an attitude.[33]

But readers – and in particular the graceless 'Mateo Luján de Sayavedra', that is, Juan Martí, author of the apocryphal *Second Part* of *Guzmán de Alfarache* (1602) – did just the opposite and used the term 'el Pícaro' to refer indiscriminately to the protagonist of the first part of the work (1599) in all his different guises: beggar, errand boy, scullion and servant. Actually Guzmanillo himself gave them a pretext for this when he admitted that the words *pícaro* and *page boy* 'are in some ways correlative and inter-changeable' (i, iii, 7; p. 409), distinct but related; and even Mateo Alemán legitimized it in the preliminaries, by alluding to the hero as 'an outcast *pícaro*' (p. 90), 'our *pícaro*' (p. 96).[34] The second part of the novel (1604) carefully avoids designating him thus; even so, many of Guzmanillo's most genuinely picaresque traits (cunning, viciousness, independence, etc.) survive in Alfarache the card-sharper, the cheat, the fraudulent merchant, the 'compliant' husband.[35] However, I do not think anyone would call him a *pícaro* on the basis of the second phase of his career alone (indeed, the first French translator distinguished the two parts by calling them *vie du Gueux* and *vie du Voleur*). And yet he still deserved the label – Alemán himself notwithstanding – in that his former roguery was still present in some respects (though increasingly diluted in others); in that he was still the same *character* that the public had called 'Pícaro' by antonomasia (and by sinechdoche, *pars pro toto*).

Thus the semantic content of the word *pícaro*, as a word made flesh in Guzmán de Alfarache and given more of an adjectival than a substantive function, was already becoming more extensive, because of the first part of the *Watchtower*, than it had been up till then: it now identified a particular individual in both the picaresque and non-picaresque aspects of his life. Although in doing so they were not really being true to Mateo Alemán (and this must be emphasized), readers used the name 'Pícaro' to refer both to Guzmán and to the *Guzmán*. For this reason, a particularly close link was seen to exist between the character and the book. And it is in relation to the 'Pícaro' of fiction – rather than to the *pícaro* of reality – that the protagonist of the picaresque novel must be seen: he is a *literary creation*, because he corresponds to the archetype of the novelistic 'Pícaro', an altogether more multi-farious, more complex type than the real *pícaro*. After Mateo Alemán (though not only because of him), the image of the *pícaro* who was to be the hero of an extended narrative had come to include a series of features – ranging from a particular type of name (so-and-so from such and such a place) and family on the one hand, to a certain way of acquiring self-consciousness, a period at university, or even a final conversion on the other – features which would never have been so commonly associated with the real, flesh-and-blood *pícaro* if Alemán had not raised this image to the level of a model.

To demonstrate all this properly would require more space and attention than are possible here. For the moment, in the absence of such detailed proof, perhaps I could offer a brief piece of indirect corroborative evidence. Several scholars have correctly pointed out a great many types and motifs that the picaresque novel has in common with pre-Lopean drama and the Golden Age *entremés*, or short theatrical interlude.[36] The *entremés*, for instance, is full of 'hungry vagabonds, waggish students, crooked innkeepers, compulsive chatterboxes, starving hidalgos puffed up with pride, quacks, ridiculous poets, thieving trollops and other types of robbers, ruffians and rogues'.[37] This is clearly the same rabble that inhabits the world of the picaresque novel. Only one figure is missing: the *pícaro* himself.

In the hotch-potch of the *entremés*, in fact, actions and characters of a picaresque type abound, but it is impossible to distinguish the *pícaro*. He cannot be identified in any individual scene or trait, whose overall effect is inevitably more characteristic of some other particular species from the list of vagabonds, wags and other types alluded to above. If he is not to become confused with this or that other sort of character, the *pícaro* needs the context, the perspective of a history, even a pre-history: that is, he needs what the novel had given him and the *entremés* could not give him.[38] On the other hand, when the *pícaro* does appear on stage, he is identifiable as such not by his dramatic presentation but by a certain novelistic feeling he conveys. If Pedro de Urdemalas, from

Cervantes's play, can be called a *pícaro*, for example, it is not because of the splendid plot in which he appears, but rather because of the long and rather untheatrical monologue in which he recounts his life, combining (and even, in places, directly echoing) the autobiographical outlines of the *Lazarillo* and the *Guzmán*.[39]

Lázaro, the pícaro and the picaresque

If the honour of first being awarded the title 'Pícaro' belongs to Guzmán, then, where do we go from there? Is *Lazarillo de Tormes* a 'picaresque novel' or not?[40] In my view, it is. Of course one looks in vain for the word *pícaro* in this little work. As I have pointed out, the term cannot have definitively acquired the meaning outlined above until the last third of the sixteenth century. But Lazarillo had more than one feature in common with the figure of the *pícaro* familiar in Spain in 1598. Let us just consider one little vignette.

At the opening of the third chapter, Lázaro, who is recovering from the wounds he suffered in Maqueda, wanders round begging in Toledo. 'As long as I was sick', he says, 'people always gave me something; but once I was well again, everyone told me: "You are a rascal and a vagabond [*bellaco y gallofero*]. Go and look for a master to serve"' (p. 101). From this brief extract alone we can be sure that everyone at the end of the century would have seen the passage in question as a thumbnail sketch of a *pícaro*. Lázaro, in fact, is presented here as a young ragamuffin, not a layabout perhaps, but at all events someone with no job or income, and available for anything: he has no reason to adopt any particular occupation, no social status to keep up, no 'accursed honour' to prevent him from living as a beggar.[41] The people of Toledo lose no time in categorizing him. Lázaro, to them, is a *bellaco*; that is, a rascal, but not just any sort of rascal: Nebrija, in 1492, had already identified the *bellaco* with the errand boy (*palangarius*), and a hundred years later, Francisco del Rosal recalled that '*bellacos* was what they used to call porters [*ganapanes*]'.[42] And if this were not enough, young Lázaro shows all the characteristics of a *gallofero*; which means (in the words of Covarrubias) 'a poor wretch... and an idler', a sham invalid, a ne'er-do-well of the type that hung around monasteries and hospitals, looking for the *gallofa*, a scrap of bread or a bowl of soup. The first thought of respectable people is to admonish such a figure and to urge him to stop being a vagrant.

Now we, of course, know that Lazarillo's plight is genuine (*et pour cause!*), that the boy feels happy when he happens to find a master, and that he will soon exchange his rags for a stable position in society. But it is no less true to say that for the moment he is wandering around waiting for something to turn up, and is free, as Alfarache puts it, to 'beg with impunity, which no honourable man can decently do' (I, iii, 4; p. 381); he has some dangerous tricks up his sleeve (as the blind man could testify, if the blow did not kill him), is as much 'addicted to wine' (p. 71) as he was little used to 'cleanliness' (p. 110), and is the very same type – in everyone's eyes – as the rascally errand boy and the false beggar. Who, in 1598, I repeat, would have failed to call him a *pícaro*? One may argue as to whether, and to what extent, he always had been a *pícaro*; but there is no doubt that he was taken to be one. That being so, did not just the same sort of thing happen to Guzmanillo?

Guzmán, as we saw just now, was *le Gueux malgré lui*. And we have just been observing that he was converted into the model hero of the picaresque novel, not as a mere reflection of the real *pícaro*, but as 'the Pícaro' of literature, an archetype which transcended the usual image of the former. The *pícaro* as a *character* is both a disposition (sometimes picaresque, sometimes perhaps not) and the pattern of a life; a pattern that is not necessarily derived from reality, but is the product of a successful novelistic formulation. Thus the hero of the picaresque is also (if I may exaggerate a little) a *narrative form and formula*.

But the fact is that this artistic form, definitively established by Mateo Alemán, can be traced directly back to the *Lazarillo*; that many of the details of which 'the Pícaro' was composed, in so far as he went beyond the *pícaro*, come from the anonymous author of the mid-sixteenth century.[43] I shall cite just a couple of brief examples, which were both decisive in the development of the genre. The *pícaro* of real life, around 1598, was seen as something quite distinct from the servant, or even the antithesis of him:

'there was an enormous gap between a *pícaro* and a page', as Guzmán himself confessed (I, iii, 7; p. 409), precisely because the former was characterized by not being obliged to 'serve or be served' (I, ii, 4; p. 276). Now Guzmán, throughout his youthful experiences (the main subject of the first part), and the protagonist of the picaresque, in most of his wanderings, are largely indistinguishable from the 'servant of many masters' (*mozo de muchos amos*).[44] Thus 'the Pícaro' parts company with the *pícaro* and follows Lazarillo. Or again, consider how important a role genealogy plays in defining the picaresque character,[45] in that a portrait of his parents often prefigures and almost invariably serves as a prologue to that of the *pícaro* himself. But the connection between the self and the family circumstances was by no means a necessary feature of the genuine *pícaro*, but rather an essentially literary element, taken over from the *Lazarillo* by Mateo Alemán.

To discuss all this more fully here would divert me from my main theme. But I would like to emphasize just one point: that such characteristics of the fictional *pícaro* do much more than simply docket him in this or that position in a system of human types; they force us to consider him in relation to a narrative structure (the series of masters is a guiding thread running through the plot: the genealogy points to a coherent and well-motivated development of the character and the argument; both involve a dialectic of stimuli and responses);[46] they imply (or rather make possible) a particular structure and identify the picaresque as *novel* (rather than real life, for example).

In defining the hero of the picaresque novel as a combination of a character and a literary pattern, we may appear to be coming perilously close to a tautology: 'The *pícaro* of the picaresque novel is the *pícaro* of the picaresque novel.' But the fact is that people recognized such a hero as a distinct entity, and realized that he was born of fiction and imitated by life (and other kinds of literature). Cervantes, who cannot have felt much sympathy for Mateo Alemán and still less for his work,[47] offers us some pertinent examples here. Precisely because of the tacit rivalry between these two creative geniuses it is all the more significant that Carriazo, in *The Illustrious Kitchen Maid*, should be characterized for us at the very outset by direct reference to Guzmanillo: 'he turned out to be such an expert in picaresque matters that he could have lectured to the famous [*pícaro*] from Alfarache'.[48] Thus the prototype was derived more from imaginative literature than from life; and for this reason it was endowed with a series of obvious artificial attributes. What Cervantes was showing us in the *pícaro* was a hybrid of reality and literature. He knew that the mixture could be improved by giving more attention to reality, but he was also aware that unless the nature of the character was to some extent dictated by literature, he stopped being a *pícaro* and became a different type – and then it was no longer a matter of 'improving', but of beginning all over again. Let us recall Ginés de Pasamonte. Ginés, a galley slave (like Guzmán) and a 'great scoundrel', had written his autobiography, *The Life of Ginés de Pasamonte*, and when Don Quixote asked him how good his book was, he declared 'It is so good . . . that it will put *Lazarillo de Tormes* and every other book of that type that ever has been or will be written in the shade. What I can tell you is that it deals with true facts, and with facts that are so delightful and amusing that no lies could equal them.'[49] Thus even a real *pícaro* such as Ginés found it necessary to compare himself with a literary model; and if *The Life of Ginés de Pasamonte* had belonged to the 'type' in question (which is not the case), it would not have been because of the 'true facts' but because of the 'lies': by virtue of its having combined, at the very least, the formula of the *Lazarillo* and the protagonist of the *Guzmán*.

When one considers the question in this light, and perceives that the *pícaro* is a literary creation, I think there can be no doubt about it: *Lazarillo de Tormes* is the first picaresque novel. The types and themes we find there were largely traditional: the blind man's boy, the squire's mischievous servant, the eternal triangle of husband, wife and lover, the funny stories, the jokes, the pardoner's tricks, and many other elements in the story were familiar features of contemporary European literature. The *Lazarillo* had selected and assembled such ingredients – odd bits and pieces from a more extensive body of picaresque *material* which was fragmentary both by its very nature and by its history – and given them unity and meaning by organizing them around a perfectly

drawn central figure.[50] The *Guzmán* blossomed out of an ident-
ical or similar repertory: the page, the errand boy (whether
idealized or not), the arts of thieving, burlesque tariffs, the
anatomy of the jail and the prison-ship, and numerous other
components of the *Watchtower of Human Life* had already, by
Alemán's period, been established literary elements for many
years.[51] But the *Guzmán* did not use the *Lazarillo* in the same way
as it used this sort of raw material, by incorporating it as a motif
or an episodic nucleus subordinated to the overall design. On
the contrary, the anonymous author of the *Lazarillo* actually
supplied him with the design itself: namely the autobiography of
a contemptible individual, structured according to a particular
pattern.

Other writers may have intuited the potential of the synthesis
set out in the *Lazarillo* (involving a character, who was the
product of a selection of details from real life and from a body of
picaresque material already existing in a variety of literary
forms, and an autobiographical form, the two of them mutually
determining each other). But it was Mateo Alemán who made
them gel into a recognizable genre which, in retrospect, proved
to have been initiated by the town crier's memoirs. An *ad hoc*
analogy may serve to clarify this: just as the first fourteen-line
poem, divided into two quatrains and two tercets, had to be
imitated at least once before it could be recognized as a fixed
verse-form – a sonnet – so the *Lazarillo* had to be imitated by the
Guzmán for the common or at least compatible features to
emerge, by the one being superimposed on the other, and for the
basic formula of the 'picaresque novel' to emerge. In this process
of superimposition, the one enriched the other. As we saw
earlier, the 'Pícaro' provided the model for the hero of the
picaresque novel, as a figure transcending the *pícaro* of reality,
largely because it reflected Lázaro de Tormes; as a result
Lázaro, in turn, was assimilated into the new character. It was a
dialectic of reciprocal influences, whereby human typology (the
delineation of the hero) was intimately allied to narrative mor-
phology. From such a dialectic, through a 'process of juxtaposi-
tion' of the *Lazarillo* and the *Guzmán* in the literary consciousness
of the time,[52] emerged the paradigm of the *picaresque novel*.

His master's voice

The picaresque novel, then, included the *Lazarillo* and the *Guzmán*, but it was not confined to either of them. Establishing it as a genre was precisely a matter of selecting some constituent elements and cementing them together, as it were, into a solid, self-sufficient framework which would be capable of standing up on its own, and therefore capable – for better or worse – of accommodating means and ends other than the original ones. On the Costa del Sol, the observant traveller will come across luxurious Swiss chalets, with high slate roofs and wooden walls, and perhaps Andalusian tiled wells and vine-covered pergolas alongside them. Of course, snow and cold weather are unknown in the area, such houses are quite incongruous in this landscape, and with local building materials only a pale imitation of the original model can be achieved. But this does not mean that these Mediterranean chalets are uninhabitable; sometimes they even possess a certain quaint charm of their own, something between 'camp' and 'kitsch'. And, above all, they free the architect from having to devise an original ground-plan and the owner from having to think how to spend his money. The same sort of thing happened with the picaresque novel, and it is significant that the first authors to turn to the new genre were Quevedo and López de Úbeda: both masters of style rather than construction, for whom the recently established model solved the problem of how to capitalize on their fabulously rich linguistic resources, by providing them with a framework on which to fashion all the disparate verbal tracery for which their talents gave them an inclination.

A moment ago I was outlining some of the characteristic features of such a framework, and incorporating them – along with certain others which I did not mention or barely touched upon – into a definition of the *pícaro* as a *genus artificiale*, a synthesis of form and substance. It would be out of place to recapitulate, let alone complete the list here. I would simply like to conclude, returning to my theme, by examining one essential feature of our picaresque character, a feature that up till now I have been taking for granted. I refer to the factor which, in principle, plays the most decisive part in turning the *pícaro* into a *literary* creation: the fact of writing his own life history.

In general terms we know the significance of the use of autobiography in *Lazarillo de Tormes* and *Guzmán de Alfarache*. In the former, first-person form created a sense of historicity to serve as a pretext for its composition – that historicity which seemed an indispensable requirement in the initial stages of the history of the novel, and which was very difficult to reconcile with such humble subject matter; it reinforced the illusion of realism; it served the purposes of a certain sort of relativism and humanism, and so on. In Alemán's book it made the 'life' and 'opinions' of the imaginary author fully compatible with each other, turning even his most tortuous disquisitions into genuinely novelistic elements; it made the plot and the various theses reinforce one another, demonstrating the didactic message as lived experience; it led to a profound exploration and revelation of the hero's innermost self. In both works, the effect of all the principal constituent elements was to account for the hero's ultimate situation, one of the most important features of which was the very fact of writing an autobiography: the main basic narrative elements of the work as a whole gave an account of the protagonist in his capacity as narrator, justifying the perspective which, in turn, determined the very existence and the content of the memoirs so that the novel, overall, was a perfectly closed structure. In both works, autobiography presented the whole of reality in terms of a particular point of view.

But that same autobiographical form, which had been so carefully elaborated and so significant in the *Lazarillo* and the *Guzmán*, became ossified, as it were, when it came to be incorporated into the archetype of the picaresque novel as a genre. It was now available for anyone to use; it could either be embodied in an organism as vital and coherent as that devised by its two precursors, or it could be used as a mere conventional prop, a framework on which to hang various trimmings which, however superficially impressive, were inappropriate or at best unnecessary. And it must be said that of these two possibilities the more prevalent proved to be the second: the use of autobiography as a mere rag-bag, with a disparate set of contents that do not fit inside, like a frame separated from its picture, or a hatbox used to keep shoes in.

Let us pause for just a moment and look at that highly complex work *El libro de entretenimiento de la pícara Justina* (The Entertaining Book of the *Pícara* Justina) (Medina del Campo, 1605), by the *licenciado* Francisco López de Úbeda.[53] Right from the prologue, indeed from the very frontispiece, the memory of Lázaro de Tormes makes its presence felt. But the figure which had a really profound influence on this work was Guzmán de Alfarache. Justina is a *pícara*, pure and simple, in that she is a female version of the 'Pícaro' (and in the future López de Úbeda planned for her, Guzmán's wife as well), and arrogates to herself a congenital form of roguery, supposedly hers 'from birth' ('desde labinición', 1, 77), which aims to put Guzmanillo's merely contingent roguery in the shade;[54] in order to achieve this, however, the author had to start from the constituent elements of the *pícaro* as a literary *character*, and greatly accentuate the importance of the family background, for example. But if López de Úbeda sometimes follows Alemán's example felicitously and creatively, at other times he retains only the most superficial aspects of material derived from the *Watchtower*, without properly appreciating its original function and significance, or even attempting to rework it to suit his own purposes.

Nowhere is this more clearly perceptible than in his use of autobiography. Marcel Bataillon, to whom we owe a series of masterly studies of the novel,[55] has very properly emphasized this point: 'The doctor and buffoon López de Úbeda takes a few autobiographical patterns or pretexts from Alemán purely as a vehicle to support his own exercises in virtuosity. And so whilst the *pícaro*, after his conversion, writes his memoirs in the galleys, Justina, the incorrigible cynic, would have us believe that she is narrating her early life from the perspective of a woman past her prime, who is on the point of embarking on a third marriage: her wedding with Guzmán himself. But one has only to read the introduction, "La melindrosa escribana" ("The Capricious Female Scribe"), which contains a series of reminiscences of Mateo Alemán's preliminaries ... to get the impression that the classic "picaresque novel" has furnished our author with no more than a framework ... For the reader, seeing an overall analogy between The *"Pícara" Justina* and the *"Pícaro" Guzmán de Alfarache* ... was the more amusing for the fact that in doing so he discovered that the false copy contained a completely different body of material ...'[56] In fact, autobiography in The *'Pícara' Justina* is an absurd sham. It neither constitutes a necessary corollary of the other elements of the book (character, plot, intention ...) nor adds any meaning to them; to use a familiar phrase, it is simply an empty shell.

Of course, the more the first person loses its true meaning, the more that highly skilful manipulation of viewpoint, which was central to the *Lazarillo* and the *Guzmán*, disappears. We should not let ourselves be deceived by statements such as the one Justina inflicts on us when discussing her time in León: 'I want to give you a very full account not so much of what I saw in León as of how I saw it, because I have made up my mind that I want people to read my soul; for the fact is that I have set myself up as a writer, and if I failed to do this much I would not be doing my job' (II, 137). In the *Lazarillo*, to convey 'what I saw' and 'how I saw it' was consistent with the nature of the protagonist, and objects were revealed to us only through the changing eye of the subject. The *Guzmán*, adopting the same approach, explored the innermost features of the imaginary narrator: to read any page here was indeed to read his 'soul'. But in The *'Pícara' Justina* this consciousness of seeing and writing, which is brought to the reader's attention explicitly and at length, can be attributed neither to the heroine nor to the supposed authoress, for there is nothing to justify it. In Justina (a figure whose incoherence is of almost outrageous proportions) the roles of 'observer' and 'writer' (ibid.) are just two more odd patches tacked on to a character which, even without them, would still be a chaotic hotch-potch cobbled together from miscellaneous features of various human types. The common denominator of the book is the way in which the narrative is diluted with affectations ('melindres'), delightful comic anecdotes ('dulces facecias'), similes, nicknames, little conceits, stories, digressions, fables, hieroglyphs, humanistic topics, rhetorical erudition, innumerable proverbs ... But neither the stylistic mode nor the perspective – nor even the one playing the part of the other – has anything at all to do with Justina: they belong to López de Úbeda alone.

Indeed, the author hardly bothers to conceal the fact. Just as he peppers the margins with annotations and frames the chapters with poems and 'improving precepts', so he devotes little attention to maintaining the consistency of the autobiographical illusion. It is Justina, for instance, to whom speeches such as the following are attributed, and, what is more, this one occurs when she is being presented in the very act of writing her memoirs: 'I wrote this little work a thousand years ago; for that time, it was more than sufficient and if it were not for certain young lads, for whose sake I couldn't bring myself to throw away all these conserves, this little book would already have gone to the spicery of its own accord. They tell me the little picarish book tastes good . . .'* ('Mil años ha que hice esta obrecilla; para aquel tiempo, sobraba, y si no fueran mocitos, que de lástima no me han dejado vaciar esta conserva, ya hubiera este librito ídose por su pie a la especería. Dícenme que está muy bueno el librito picarero . . .'). But López de Úbeda only intends to deceive us up to a point, and with a gesture towards childish pronunciation, he hastens to add 'But dear me, I woz forgettin' I'm a woman and my name is Justina' ('Mas, ay, que se me olvidaba que ero mujer y me llamo Justina', I, 49–50).

I do not want to give the impression that I am detracting from the merits of López de Úbeda's extraordinary book (both extraordinary and very modern, in the context of the current boom in the American novel; it is always as imaginative and tortuous stylistically, sometimes as learnedly obscene and often as incomprehensible as the *Paradiso*, to name but one example). This perpetual ambiguity of the narrative first person, which would have destroyed a work like *Guzmán de Alfarache*, can generate a particular level of meaning in *The 'Pícara' Justina*, albeit a distinctly secondary level.[57] It can, for instance, be taken to indicate the presence of other ambiguities of context. Marcel Bataillon has seen the novel as being full of enigmatic keys, of concealed

---

* [*Translator's note*. The Spanish is obscure here. 'Going to the spicery' probably refers to the practice of using pages of unwanted books to make little paper packets for spices. But for popular demand, Justina's book would have been consigned to oblivion, used as scrap paper.]

references to contemporary court life; and he has suggested that well-informed readers of the period must have read the novel on two levels at once, savouring the *double entendre*. Now if Bataillon is right (as he usually is), then perhaps the obvious disguise of the first person serves to indicate that a number of persons, places and things are also present in disguise, thereby preparing the reader for the enjoyable exercise of unmasking them. Unfortunately that is not my subject here. I was concerned merely to ascertain what use López de Úbeda made of the main precepts of the newly established poetics of the picaresque genre. The most cursory of comparisons makes the answer quite obvious: in the *Lazarillo* and the *Guzmán*, autobiography, which went hand in hand with the realist aim and the various implied 'theses' of the work in question, incorporated all the various material (plan, character, style) into a single point of view. In *The 'Pícara' Justina*, autobiography lacked any essential function and, for the very reason that it was soon found to be redundant, it made the lack of any real connection between the various elements of the work even more glaring: it was just an empty imitation.

The same questions produce the same answers in the case of another work of genius – and very bad picaresque novel: *La vida del Buscón, llamado don Pablos* (The Life of the Cheat, called Don Pablos),[58] a very early work (of around 1604)[59] by Francisco de Quevedo. Quevedo raided the stock of elements which constituted the genre, intent on competing with the anonymous sixteenth-century author and with the sombre Alemán, and outdoing them by the sheer incisive power of his ingenuity. But Quevedo's was a critical, analytical intellect, inventive 'only ... at the level of the conceit and of language',[60] prone to dissipate its efforts on details rather than concentrating on a comprehensive treatment of themes and problems. One has only to consider his other comic works, both those contemporary with the *Buscón* (*Vida de la corte* [Life at Court], *Libro de todas las cosas* [Book about Everything There Is], and so on) and those of a later period (the last *Sueños* [Visions], *La hora de todos* [The Hour of All Men]). These really are collections of disparate fragments, patchwork: isolated observations, individual vignettes, miscellaneous incidents, always open to grafting or pruning, and often linked together only by being vaguely connected with a given subject and, of course, by their astonishing stylistic execution. In Quevedo, even the favourite technique of the portrait involves breaking the figure up into a 'mosaic of disembodied objects' (as Leo Spitzer pointed out), scarcely, if at all, under the control of any unifying principle.[61] It is not surprising, then, that when he tried his hand at the picaresque, virtually everything about this type of writing that made it a *novel*, a construct, escaped him; that having recognized the essential characteristics of the genre, he took them over as a series of discrete fragments without perceiving (or at any rate without attempting to adapt or to recreate) their underlying relationship with each other.

The use of the autobiographical pattern here is once again revealing. In the first place, why does Pablos write? We have not the slightest idea. It is true that at the beginning of some manuscripts one finds a brief 'Dedicatory Letter': 'Having learned of Your Worship's desire to hear about the various episodes of my life, I have decided, in order that no one else should tell lies about them (as has happened to others), to send you this account, which will do much to relieve you during your sad moments . . .' (p. 11). This little passage is of doubtful authenticity, and is unquestionably not part of the original version. But let us suppose it is genuine. In that case, who is 'His Worship' and why should he be interested in Pablos's memoirs? There is no way of finding the answer.

Perhaps there would not even be any point in raising the question if the *Lazarillo* had not existed and if Quevedo were not plainly copying one of its techniques. Another 'Your Worship' – we met him earlier – had written to the town crier of Toledo asking him to give a full and detailed account of 'the case' which everyone was talking about and which was the basis of their relationship; and Lázaro's answer had been to select those episodes from his past that would throw most light on the present 'case', which intrigued 'His Worship'. Thus in the *Lazarillo*, the addressee was a central focus of the narrative; in the final analysis, 'His Worship' explained the existence and the structure of the autobiography. That is why the narrator frequently addressed him. If, for example, Lázaro introduced his portrait of his family with the phrase 'Well then, Your Worship should know ... ', he did so in order to indicate that his origins had a great deal to do with 'the case' under discussion; that, for instance, if Antona Pérez had taught him to 'associate with good people', he had followed this advice by associating with the Archpriest, 'my master, and Your Worship's servant and friend'.

But in the *Buscón*, what lies behind the initial apostrophe ('I, *Sir*, am from Segovia') and the other appeals to His Worship? We don't know; they mean nothing to us. We are not even entitled to take them as vague references to the reading public in general.[62] The 'Dedicatory Letter' puts this beyond doubt: 'Having learned of *Your Worship's desire* to hear about the various episodes of my life ... '. It sounds like the opening of the *Guzmán*: 'The desire that I had, curious reader, to tell you my life history ... '. Here everything is fully accounted for: it is Alfarache who wishes to relate his own story, out of a desire to serve a didactic function, and who makes a 'general confession' to his readers, continually addressing them, because the main object of his book is to influence them, and everything in it is directed towards that didactic end. In the *Buscón* there is no equivalent – except on the most superficial level – for the town crier's 'Your Worship' or the galley slave's 'curious reader': in no way does Pablos's 'Sir' form any real part of the novel – it is just a name. Quevedo found it in the basic vocabulary of the picaresque, included it in his book and did not trouble to give it any real meaning (neither the substance nor even the shadow of a personality). In this way the addressee, who had previously been a fundamental element of autobiography, was reduced to a superflous nonentity, which might as well – or better – have been left out altogether: and this amounted to a crime against art itself.

Let us leave His Worship to one side and return to our original question. Why does Pablos write? He has no motive outside himself for doing so, of the sort Lázaro has. Or, alternatively, he fails to express such a motive in narrative form: for it was not enough to state the motive; it had to be effectively incorporated into the autobiography. Does he perhaps have that taste for introspection, for looking backwards and inwards, that distinguishes Guzmanillo from the very outset and makes him an organic extension of Alfarache, who is writing his memoirs? Of course not. There is no getting round the fact that you cannot look at what is not there.

The fact is that Pablos hardly has any 'inner life' at all, apart from his digestive processes. The inconsistency of the character verges on the absurd; although of course the absurd, as an aesthetic mode, is as respectable as realism or more so. The biographical pattern to which the novelistic *pícaro* usually conformed involved a series of changes of fortune and occupation. The anonymous author of the *Lazarillo*, and Mateo Alemán, had managed to include such changes while at the same time maintaining the *decorum* of the protagonist (as verisimilitude of character was formerly known). Certain incidents entailed certain attitudes, new flashes of insight were followed by particular actions; the interplay between the self and his circumstances took place along a clear, unbroken line of evolution. Quevedo retained the main landmarks from this route, but not what connected them with each other. Here again, he reduced the form to an empty shell, devoid of the content that had made it or was capable of making it relevant. For example, if the apocryphal Guzmán's master had been a nuns' gallant then Pablos has got to follow suit; Quevedo will force him to become a platonic lover, for all that he may earlier have made him insist that 'I don't want women ... except to go to bed with' (ii, 7; p. 228), and so on. It would be easy to catch Pablos blatantly contradicting himself time and time again. Ultimately he is little more than a puppet,[63] whose basic function is to provide a pretext for a miscellaneous succession of sarcastic witticisms.[64] There is nothing wrong with this in principle: the term *novel*, like Aristotle's *being*, can have many different meanings,[65] and the unrealistic nature of the Buscón seems, as I have said, quite as legitimate as the most orthodox naturalism. The trouble is that in adopting the basic model of the picaresque and divesting it of those elements that had made it work properly, Quevedo did not tackle the problem of creating a form of his own, and broke the novel up into a series of unconnected planes.

Let us, however, consider Pablos's one relatively consistent feature: his desire for honour and social superiority. 'His mother was a witch, his father a thief and his uncle a hangman, and he himself was the most contemptible, evil-natured wretch in the whole of creation' (III, 7; p. 230). But this crook is actuated precisely by the 'aim of becoming a gentleman' (I, 2; p. 31) and of escaping from the disgrace of his family background. A considerable part of his career is devoted to a determined attempt to aim 'higher' (I, 7; p. 94), and to wipe away all trace of the ignominious origins with which he is saddled.[66] Thus if there is one definite feature in Pablos's personality it is the objective of 'repudiating his heredity' (II, 5; p. 148). But that being so, can such an objective possibly be reconciled with the writing of an autobiography of this sort, the whole of which testifies unequivocally to the abject, ignominious nature of the supposed author? I think not. Because of course there is nothing even to suggest that the *pícaro* has changed or ever will change. The novel ends precisely by pointing out that the very opposite is true: the Buscón sets out for the Indies, 'and there' he says, 'things went worse for me, as Your Worship will see in the Second Part, because no one ever rises in the world just by a change of scene, without a change in his life and habits' (III, 10; p. 280). Might the uncertainty have been resolved in the unwritten Second Part? We'll believe that when we see it ... One thing, at any rate, is clear enough: in the book as it stands there is not even the remotest attempt to give novelistic expression to the indispensable transition from Pablos as actor to Pablos as author. And without such an attempt, the use of the first person is at best superfluous – mere lip-service to tradition.

Quevedo did not really understand the *Lazarillo* (much as he admired it) or the *Guzmán*. He did not understand that the town crier and the galley slave narrate the past in order to clarify the present (and, in doing so, to account for the very act of narration).[67] He did not understand the consummate ambiguity with which Lázaro offers his book as a kind of deposition in his own defence (even though we, by putting ourselves outside the character, could read it as an indictment), nor that the harshness with which Guzmán presents himself as unworthy and evil confirms his repentance and the whole process of his conversion: his entire life. Quevedo was not bothered by the radical inconsistency involved in Pablos writing the sort of memoirs he is supposed to be writing, in which his credibility as protagonist and as narrator is systematically undermined. A constant feature of the whole work, in fact, is the way in which the Buscón is forced, inexplicably, to denounce himself out of his own mouth, just to provide an opportunity for a joke – Quevedo's joke.

We need look no further than the first paragraph, and consider the *pícaro*'s own words: 'They say [my father] was of good stock, and considering the way he drank you can quite believe it' (I, I, p. 15). Lázaro would simply have hinted: 'They say he was of good stock.' But Pablos does not appreciate subtleties of this sort, which make the *Lazarillo* a masterpiece of ironic truth. He is determined to spell everything out for us, and hastens to elaborate on the joke with a gloss that makes it quite clear, even at the expense of destroying any claim to verisimilitude that his avowed intention of 'repudiating his heredity' might have had. This is typical of him both as author and character. Consider the following glaring example. When he is dressed up as the 'cock of the walk' (*rey de gallos*) in the Carnival, wearing a hat covered with feathers, and the coarse market women and boys pelt him with 'colossal carrots, titanic turnips, aubergines and other vegetables', as would have happened if he had been a witch led out for public humiliation, Pablos began to shout: 'Good women, although I'm wearing feathers, I'm not Aldonza de San Pedro, my mother' ('Hermanas, aunque llevo plumas, no soy Aldonza de San Pedro, mi madre', I, 2; pp. 28–9). How absurd! Quite funny – at least if one likes that sort of thing – but unbelievable. Nobody would say such a thing in that situation, least of all Pablos.[68] The only voice we can hear in this passage is his master's. The punch line itself, and still more the merciless relish with which it is formulated – the adversative *aunque* ('although'), the specific mention of forename and surname, the explicit reminder of the family relationship – must be attributed to Don Francisco de Quevedo alone: they could not conceivably be the Buscón's own words.

Here again, there is no need to cite a whole series of examples. The conclusion, to my mind, is beyond doubt: it never even occurred to Quevedo to observe Pablos's point of view consistently. The following extended passage by Fernando Lázaro is worth quoting here:

The young Quevedo, either by instinct or through the irresistible attraction of the *Guzmán*, had discovered the underworld. Living, as he was, within a social system with a set of beliefs which he found satisfactory, or which it was in his interests to respect, he considered anything that did not conform to that system to be fair game for his sarcasm. From the standpoint of his own unshakeable principles of honour and lineage, the destitute, the outcasts from human society are all mere nonentities. Quevedo's world is properly constituted, the other is not: it is as simple as that. Nevertheless, there is much in it for an observer contemplating it from a distance to enjoy: 'I confess that for a long time – for I had stopped some distance away to watch him – I thought he was a magician, and I almost decided not to go on.' 'Bosch never painted such strange contortions as the ones I saw.' 'Finally I placed myself where I could and the different attitudes of the lovers were so peculiar that they were a sight worth seeing.' Pablos is constantly stepping outside the action in order to observe it: '*they sat down* to eat . . . I would rather not say what *we ate* . . .', or rather, in order that the novelist may observe it, without ever getting fully involved in that world, the attraction, for him, lying not in what may actually happen, but in what he chooses to see or intuits. In this way, the structure of that peripheral society disintegrates, its internal nexus disappears and it is linked instead, by a series of radial connections, to the author.[69]

Exactly so. And it would not greatly matter, for instance, that Don Francisco makes Pablos narrate things that the latter cannot possibly know,[70] were it not for the fact that at the same time such inconsistencies reveal that the book was not conceived as an artistically unified whole, with each element depending on the others. Let us qualify this apparently categorical statement by reminding ourselves that we have examined the *Buscón* exclusively in terms of the theoretical 'precepts' of the picaresque novel. But why did Quevedo have to observe these precepts so slavishly in superficial ways, if he was not then going to recreate them to form an original system? In particular, why adopt the autobiographical form and then turn it into an inorganic, aesthetically superfluous excrescence? It is difficult to avoid suspecting him of plagiarism.

The tragicomedy of the picaresque novel

With *The 'Pícara' Justina* and *The Life of the Buscón*, the picaresque novel had entered a dead-end street.[71] The formula deduced from the *Lazarillo* and the *Guzmán*, when applied in a mechanical way, without any underlying structural foundation, seemed over-predictable, merely monotonous. Such a formula, now isolated as an abstract system, was not obtrusive in the *Lazarillo* and the *Guzmán*, concealed as it was behind the richly developed characterization of the protagonist; in *Justina* and the *Buscón*, by contrast, it eclipsed the character. Since the structural bond provided by the hero's progressive life history (involving not only *what* happens but *whom* it happens to) had constituted the main attraction for the reader, once he had lost his distinctive individuality the picaresque had little to offer that had not already been available in other literary areas for a long time.[72] And it ceased to be interesting.

So much so that the *Buscón* itself, which first circulated in manuscript, was not printed until long after it was completed, at a more favourable time when the genre had come back into fashion; and fifteen years passed, after Quevedo had finished it, before another genuine picaresque novel appeared. Between 1605 and 1620, however, the *pícaro* popped up more than once in different types of writing (whether narrative or otherwise) from those in which he was first introduced to the world as a literary creation. In 1612, for instance, Alonso Jerónimo de Salas Barbadillo published *La hija de Celestina* (Celestina's Daughter).[73] This little work, thoroughly respectable as regards style and construction, relates the execution and immediate consequences of a fraud perpetrated by three villains (Helena, la Méndez and Montúfar), ending with a brief appendix on the subsequent fate of all those who take part in the plot. Well now, within the framework of this single action, there is a speech lasting several pages from Helena, the daughter of Pierres and Celestina, in which she tells Montúfar about her shameful, sinful 'birth and origins', in the manner of Guzmán or Justina. Seven years later, a certain mysterious doctor named Carlos García brought out a work in Paris entitled *La desordenada codicia de los bienes ajenos* (The Disordered Covetousness of Other Men's Goods):[74] itself a disordered though entertaining collection of curiosities and fantasies about the criminal under-world ('the misery of prison life', 'the nobility and excellence of stealing', 'thieves' statutes and laws', and so on), interspersed with the autobiography of Andrés, master of the 'thieving profession'.

In my opinion, neither *Celestina's Daughter* nor *The Disordered Covetousness of Other Men's Goods* can really be called 'picaresque novels' if we want the term to retain any effective meaning. It is true that in both books the *pícaro* of the picaresque novel appears, but only in the way he appears in *Urdemalas* or the short stories of Cervantes.[75] If it is legitimate to call Helena and Andrés *pícaros* – rather than just a delinquent prostitute and a thief – this is not because of the general overall construction of the works in which they figure, but because of a secondary, inessential element in that construction. Our *pícaro* (not to be confused, as we know by now, with the *pícaro* of real life) first appeared in conjunction with a certain narrative pattern, and this synthesis had the ability to organize many types of material, which had previously existed only as unconnected episodic fragments, into a unified structure. Salas Barbadillo and Carlos García reverse the process that led to the birth of the genre: they squeeze the original pattern down to one episode and insert it into a structure drawn from the very tradition which the very first picaresque novels were aiming to transcend. So *Celestina's Daughter* includes Helena's autobiographical tale within a fragmentary *novella* plot, in the style of Boccaccio or Bandello, just the sort of plot that the author of the *Lazarillo* and Alemán had amalgamated into the life of the protagonist (or interpolated as a digression pure and simple). *The Disordered Covetousness of Other Men's Goods* records Andrés's speech as just another in the series of individual fragments of which the book is composed: anatomies of prison life, catalogues of scoundrels and burlesque laws, very much the sort of thing that Alemán had gleaned from the literary scene of his own time and woven into the story of Alfarache.[76] When the matter is viewed in this light, will it seem excessively narrow on my part to argue that such works (and others like them)[77] should be excluded from the canon of the picaresque novel? They might be called 'narratives with a *pícaro*', but they run directly counter to the principles of composition which created the original design of the picaresque.

That this assessment is correct is confirmed when one observes how faithfully (if not successfully) Juan Cortés de Tolosa's *Laz-*

arillo de Manzanares[78] and Juan de Luna's *Second Part of Lazarillo de Tormes*[79] return to the original design fifteen years after the *Buscón*. 1620 was an important year, as regards visible activity, in the history of the picaresque. The genre had been discovered and temporarily played out between 1599 and 1605; in an exactly parallel period, between 1620 and 1626, it was to undergo a sort of renaissance. At just the same time as the works of Cortés de Tolosa and Juan de Luna, in fact, no fewer than three editions of the original *Lazarillo* came out, as well as a new reprint of the *Guzmán*, a few months earlier, in 1619, that would serve as the basis for all subsequent editions.[80] Then from 1624 to 1626, Jerónimo de Alcalá Yáñez brought out the two parts of *Alonso, mozo de muchos amos* (Alonso, Servant of Many Masters).[81] And this same year, 1626, saw the appearance of the *Varia fortuna del soldado Píndaro* (Various Adventures of the Soldier Píndaro), by Gonzalo de Céspedes y Meneses and, finally, the publication of *The Life of the Buscón*.

It is worth drawing attention to this second phase of the picaresque, but this is not the place to evaluate its contributions. For my present purposes, in any case, these are of very little interest. The plain fact is that the problem of point of view scarcely arises in these second-generation writers. Hardly at all in Juan de Luna, of course, who planned to continue the auto-biography as far as the protagonist's death (*sic*), and whose preposterous Lázaro is metamorphosed into a whole series of different characters, connected only by bearing the same name. Nor to any great extent in *Lazarillo de Manzanares*, in which the hero, though admittedly not entirely out of keeping with the book (if one is charitable, one might believe it really was written by a 'pedagogue' and schoolmaster as dull as the protagonist), could fairly be called the most nondescript individual it is possible to conceive, devoid of any distinguishing human feature. It is rather more of an issue in Céspedes y Meneses, to be sure, but one must qualify this by noting that here the author has not really made Píndaro's autobiography belong within the genre of the novel itself – as was the case in the *Lazarillo* and the *Guzmán* – but rather outside it, by reference to a type of literature quite separate from the picaresque: genuine soldiers' memoirs.[82]

In fact between 1620 and 1626 Jerónimo de Alcalá Yáñez was the only author who seems to have understood that to use the basic form of the genre with any degree of artistic economy one had to establish a link between the *pícaro* as actor and the *pícaro* as author. In order to achieve this with some measure of originality, Alcalá Yáñez avoids turning Alonso into a writer and has him relate his life orally. The first part takes the form of a dialogue between the protagonist and the sub-abbot of the monastery which he has chosen to enter as a *donado*, or unprofessed servant; in the second he has become a hermit, and converses with an old acquaintance, the priest of San Zoles. We are not surprised to find that in both cases he is a penitent: an unstable character, as full of good intentions as he is lacking in will-power, who has gone through life alternating between sin and repentance in almost equal proportions. Nor are we surprised by the innumerable disquisitions, anecdotes and other paraphernalia with which he peppers his biographical story: for the fact is that he always was an irrepressible chatterbox, rightly or wrongly – posterity has dubbed him 'el donado hablador' ('the talkative *donado*') – and the verbosity and taste for preaching he displays as a narrator got him into trouble more than once as a character.[83] In this book, then, point of view is somewhat tentatively embodied in novelistic form, to a certain limited extent. But it is obvious that Alcalá Yáñez is following Mateo Alemán's recipe without coming anywhere near him as regards talent: the portrait of Alonso is too often indistinctly drawn, the link between the 'life' and the 'opinions' is never established with the same unfailing pertinence as in *Guzmán de Alfarache*, everything seems insipid and out of focus... Jerónimo de Alcalá's attempt, though respectable in its context, fails simply for lack of genius. It was not enough to recognize in someone else's work those features that were capable of giving life to the archetype of the picaresque, and then try to apply them to one's own: without the same literary gifts, such features themselves turned into lifeless formulae. Good critics can make mediocre writers.

After 1626 the picaresque novel only cropped up occasionally and fortuitously. An *homme de lettres* (and even *polygraphe*) like Alonso de Castillo Solórzano[84] tried his hand at the genre with *La niña de los embustes*, *Teresa de Manzanares* (The Girl Trickster, Teresa de Manzanares) (1632), and, for the purposes of our enquiry, the experiment is completely unsuccessful. Here the use of autobiography is so gratuitous that the author, who was after all an intelligent literary craftsman, switched over much more happily to the conventional third person when he came to use the figure of the *pícaro* again. The results of this desertion of the first person, the *Aventuras del bachiller Trapaza* (Adventures of the Bachelor Trapaza) (1637) and *La Garduña de Sevilla* (The Wildcat of Seville) (1642), might provisionally be placed in a separate sub-group within the category of 'narratives with a *pícaro*'.[85] The numerous interpolations become so prominent that they swamp the character, and it is no longer possible to regard them as dependent on a single first-person consciousness that would serve as the common denominator of the multifarious contents:[86] at least *pro forma*, for in the final analysis only form is capable of identifying a literary species. Nor, it would seem, can any greater significance be ascribed to the use of first-person form in the incoherent *Vida de don Gregorio Guadaña* (Life of Don Gregorio Guadaña) (1644), one of the two prose texts by Antonio Enriquez Gómez which complement his verse work *El siglo pitagórico* (The Pythagorean Age); it was doubtless intended to be completed in a separate volume.[87]

The last legitimate son of the picaresque family (and in some ways one of the healthiest), *La vida y hechos de Estebanillo González, hombre de buen humor* (The Life and Deeds of Estebanillo González, Man of Merry Humour) (1646), is of only peripheral concern to us here. Concealed behind Estebanillo stands an anonymous author reconstructing a real-life existence[88] in literary terms, and in terms of a specific tradition of buffoonery (with a cynicism which Professor Parker finds 'particularly unpleasant' and Juan Goytisolo finds 'exemplary').[89] In fact Covarrubias's definition of the *truhán* ('merry-andrew', or 'buffoon', as we would now say) offers us an almost exact biography and character sketch of Estebanillo: 'A clownish wag, without shame, without honour or respect. This type of person, with the characteristics stated above, is admitted to the palaces of kings and to the houses of great lords, and he is free to say whatever he wants, although it is true that he ultimately pays for all his liberties by being ill-treated in innumerable ways, and he endures all this out of gluttony and avarice, for he is very well fed, and when he feels the time is ripe, he retires as a very wealthy man.'[90] We know hardly anything about the 'liberal art' of 'buffoonery' (II, 39),[91] because, not surprisingly, it rarely took written form; the author of the prologue to the novel even maintains that Estebanillo was 'the first person' to 'be both a joker and an author' (I, 53). But we do get some idea of the buffoon's style – speaking *disparates* ('nonsense') and telling *bernardinas* ('boastful lies'), for instance – as well as perhaps the main subject of his jokes: himself. Indeed, Covarrubias indicates as much when he puts the emphasis on the *truhán* as a 'man ... without honour', and it is confirmed by other accounts which suggest a close connection between this figure and the medieval jongleur and modern clown,[92] both of whom are also experts at telling ridiculous stories against themselves.

But beyond this, Estebanillo's 'jokes' are a tissue of reminiscences of Spanish Golden Age literature (Góngora, Lope, Quevedo, Pérez de Montalbán and a long list of lesser writers). Would it be fair to say, then, that he was bound to use the model of the picaresque novel? For what other long-established literary form was better suited to the favourite subject matter and style of buffoonery? The social position of the supposed author solved at a stroke the problem of self-disparagement – of the *pícaro* using himself as the object of his own ridicule and contempt – a problem which, as we have seen, confounded no less a writer than Quevedo, to name only the most distinguished example. Was it not inevitable that a book by a buffoon well versed in seventeenth-century literature would graft itself on to the picaresque and give it an injection of new blood, by now too late to save it?· It is precisely on that level, at that intersection of two traditions, that an explanation of the consistency of point of view and the true meaning of autobiography in *Estebanillo González* can be found.

It is time to finish. I am sorry, of course, to have dwelt so much (or so little) on the last gasps of the picaresque. Ours is a tragic story. And I call it *tragic* because – as Dante would say – 'in principio est admirabilis et quieta, in fine ... est foetida et horribilis': because it has an unhappy ending. But on the other hand, it would not be inappropriate to call it *comic*, if one revives one of the possible meanings the adjective once held.

Let me explain. From the Middle Ages up till the eighteenth century (if I may put it as vaguely as that, so as to avoid having to embark on a mass of highly involved qualifications) it was normally held that the status of a literary work was determined by the social status of its protagonists, '*ratione personarum*'.[93] So the hierarchy of genres and styles reflected the class hierarchy in a society which was based firmly on differences of birth. As a matter of principle, then, the tone and dignity of a work of fiction were inseparable from the level of society on which its action took place. The characters were conceived as types, and it was not possible, for example, to treat a low (*humilis*) character in an elevated (*gravis*) style, which was reserved for important, august personages ('gravis gravibus personis').[94] In particular, the common people were debarred from entering literature with the fully rounded personalities they possessed in real life. They were only admitted if they were reduced to a single pejorative facet, to provide the opportunity for a joke or an insult. Noblemen and magnates could afford the luxury of a complex personality; peasants had to be content, in almost all cases, with being one-dimensional, especially one-dimensionally ridiculous. And since humour – as Cristóbal Suárez de Figueroa was well aware – 'must necessarily be generated by lowly men',[95] the domain of comedy was, with very few exceptions, reserved exclusively for them.

And this explains the fate of the picaresque novel. Recognizing it as a genre meant just that: confining it to this domain of comedy; specifying the identity of its protagonist precluded devoting one's complete artistic attention to him. We know that this is not what happened in *Lazarillo de Tormes* or *Guzmán de Alfarache*. The anonymous author of the former may very possibly have been inspired by a certain relativism and humanism that were part of his very nature. In any event, whatever his own *Weltanschauung* may have been, whatever the reasons that led him to adopt the autobiographical form, his use of first-person narrative and presentation of the whole of reality in terms of a particular point of view enabled him to accomplish an extraordinary feat, unprecedented in prose fiction up till that time: to conceive a character as insignificant as the town crier of Toledo from within, with profound novelistic understanding. (Or perhaps the other way round: his desire to achieve such a feat led him to adopt the autobiographical structure.) Mateo Alemán declares that when faced with the life to come, at least in terms of religious belief, all men are equal and enjoy the same freedom. He portrays Guzmán de Alfarache, then, as a complete, coherent individual, presenting him as the equal of anyone and bestowing the same freedom on him, quite independently of all conventional stereotypes. Alemán, too, constructs his character from within and, disregarding the precepts of the theorists, even endows him with certain tragic characteristics. In Alfarache, autobiography goes hand in hand with autonomy; strict adherence to first-person form, to the point of view of actor and author, is more than a mere rhetorical device: it is a sign of Guzmán's full independence, of his integrity, in both human and aesthetic terms.

But as I have said, reducing *Lazarillo de Tormes* and *Guzmán de Alfarache* to a formula, extracting a prescription from the two books that could then, as it were, be made up to order in the literary pharmacy of the time, involved incorporating the genre into the comic style and, by definition, conceiving the *pícaro* from the outside. This, in fact, is what actually happened, a point clearly apparent from even the most cursory examination of narrative point of view in works later than Alemán's *Watchtower*, revealing as it does the grossly inadequate way in which autobiographical form is used in them. All the same, things could hardly have been otherwise. The only way the picaresque could survive as a genre of this sort, as an archetype, was by operating within the system laid down by traditional poetics. But its very birth within this system signalled the death of its originality. The fate of the picaresque was to misunderstand the lesson of the author of the *Lazarillo* and of Mateo Alemán, and to return to class prejudice and everything that that implied as regards the hierarchy of literature. *The Life of the Buscón* is admirable evidence of this, because it follows its models so closely and is so distinguished a work in other respects:[96] there, presenting Pablos as an object of constant contempt and ridicule, confining him to a single pejorative facet, really does amount to presenting him as a member of a social class,[97] as a type. The picaresque, I repeat, had entered a dead-end street.

But where would it have led had it followed in the footsteps of the *Lazarillo* and the *Guzmán*? Straight towards the modern novel. Whether we like it or not, the history of the modern novel, until quite recently, is the history of a certain type of realist novel, which is based on nothing more nor less than a rejection of the doctrine of the hierarchy of styles[98] and characterized by the conviction that every sort of subject matter and character is worthy of the same literary attention. Of course, in Habsburg Spain, the picaresque novel, as a whole, was unable to achieve all this. But to have intuited the possibility of it constitutes the unique genius of *Lazarillo de Tormes* and *Guzmán de Alfarache*.[99]

Postscript

The present book might perhaps serve to illustrate the notion that literature is an ever-changing compromise between form and history, between internal factors and elements extrinsic to the text, between creation and criticism. It did not arise out of any desire to study the *technique* of 'point of view' in the abstract, as a category of an atemporal 'rhetoric of fiction', and then to trace it through the corpus of the 'Spanish picaresque novel'. It derives its *raison d'être*, its methods of analysis and its historical perspective from the establishment of one simple formal fact: the main unifying principle of *Lazarillo de Tormes* and *Guzmán de Alfarache* lies in the subordination of all their constituent elements to the particular point of view of the protagonist and fictitious author.

A fundamental theme of both novels is precisely the gradual formation of this point of view: both of them *relate* how the *pícaro* ends up becoming a writer, why he is composing his auto-biography, what experiences and what features of his disposition determine the selection and arrangement of the very episodes he recounts, the manner and the language in which he presents them, the meaning he infuses into them or ascribes to them... Thus plot, structure, narrative technique, style and 'message' are always phases or versions of Lázaro's or Guzmán's point of view. So much so, that to isolate and define such components in the *Lazarillo* and the *Guzmán* is an even more odiously banal exercise than in the case of other masterpieces. The great achievement of our two novels lies to a large extent in the natural way in which these conventional components merge and are transformed one into another, in the facility, for example, with which the narrative technique of the *Lazarillo* makes us read this technique as a 'message' in itself (thus the fragmentation of many scenes, and indeed of the story as a whole, into several stages of perception is equivalent to an explicit conception of the world), or even with which certain linguistic details underline the overall structure of the *Guzmán* (where, for instance, the use of the second person, *tú*, in the Pícaro's interior 'monologues' is just one more aspect of the conflict between 'life' and 'opinions' which shapes the whole work). Now if these components merge in this way, they do so precisely as dimensions of a self, manifestations of the point of view of the protagonist and author.

So effective and multivalent a use of point of view to unify every factor in a narrative, so intelligent a web of correspondences geared towards the creation of a character, can probably be deemed an artistic success whatever critical standards are applied to them: in the final analysis – to put it at its lowest – they conform to certain notions of coherence and symmetry, of functional harmony and expressive 'economy', which have been almost universally valued. But this artistic success occupies a very particular place in history. Two especially pertinent historical yardsticks, in the shorter and the longer term, suggest themselves at once: the literary theories of the Renaissance and the birth of the archetypal realist novel, the realist novel of the nineteenth century. For the fact that the novel lacks a specific and unequivocal form of its own, that it appeared late and has undergone such vicissitudes (it is even debatable whether it still exists...) makes it almost impossible to discuss any novel without at the same time taking account of the whole history of the genre.

This is true of the *Lazarillo* and the *Guzmán* to a conspicuous degree. The fact is that when Lázaro and Guzmán tell the story of their lives, and tell it in terms consistent with what those lives have been and are now, we are presented for the first time in the history of European prose narrative with a sustained attempt to conceive individuals of lowly social rank *from within*. Thus the anonymous author of around 1553 and Mateo Alemán disregarded a fundamental tenet of the literary theory generally accepted at that time: the principle that the nature of characters was predetermined by the position where they belonged in the social scale, and that the fate of common people was to be treated as ridiculous caricatures, because 'lowly people', as Cascales repeated, 'are the ones who provoke laughter' (see chapter 3, n. 95). The ambiguity and good-humoured relativism of the *Lazarillo* partially concealed its rejection of this tenet: the uninhibited impudence with which the town crier of Toledo set himself up as the measure of all things and laughed at 'those who inherited noble estates' was somewhat veiled by the fact that he also came to laugh at himself. In Mateo Alemán's hands the possibilities and implications of the design of the *Lazarillo* were more openly revealed: he took this very design as a starting point and patently left the domain of comedy altogether, setting the decisive moments of Guzmán's career in a tragic key. Now in this respect, the transition (I will not say progress) from the *Lazarillo* to the *Guzmán* corresponds exactly to the path which leads from earlier types of fiction to the 'classic' novel of the realist period, with its conviction that great and small individuals deserve an equally full artistic treatment and, in the delightful words of the Goncourt brothers, that 'ce qu'on appelle "les basses classes" [a] droit au roman'.[1]

The examination of the series *Lazarillo* plus *Guzmán* leads us unmistakably in a certain direction. This book began by emphasizing that the *Lazarillo* had to disguise itself as true history and base itself on a generally accepted literary model. It was so important to maintain the illusion that Lázaro was a real person, and that his letter to His Worship was genuine, that the author even chose not to reveal his own name.[2] The fake had to be flawless: only then could a product so alien to the conventions of the period dare to appear in public, only then could Lázaro's *I* exercise its full potential. Mateo Alemán has no hesitation in putting his name to his work, and in distancing himself from the character through a series of (fundamental) prologues, which neatly define the imaginary context; he has no need to present Guzmán's autobiography as real, it is enough for him that it should be plausible; and his ideas as to the modality which he is cultivating are perfectly clear: 'poetic history' (*Tom Jones*, in the 1740s, still calls itself an 'heroic, *historical*, prosaic *poem*'), 'fictional history' ('historia fabulosa').[3] Continuing along the path opened up around 1553, we enter a sphere in which the form of the

Lazarillo is infused with a new spirit: the particular nature of a story of that type becomes recognizable,[4] the laws by which the *fiction* operates are firmly established. But the recognition of those particular laws was precisely the innovation which led to the full flowering of the modern novel and gave it its guarantee of respectability. The step from the *Lazarillo* to the *Guzmán* is analogous to the process which gradually took place in eighteenth-century France and England: 'From novels which claim to be literally true (and are often wildly implausible [for all that they call themselves memoirs or rigorously historical letters]), there is a trend towards works laying less emphasis on their supposedly factual origin, and displaying instead more concern for everyday standards of probability and possibility.'[5] It is scarcely necessary to recall that when this trend reaches its culmination we find ourselves with what actually called itself *le siècle du roman*.

For present purposes the couple of examples I have just suggested will suffice, although it would be possible to cite many others which lead us to exactly the same conclusion: the successive achievements of the *Lazarillo* and the *Guzmán* mark out a line of development whose direction is comparable to the process of gestation of what is usually considered the classic realist novel, that of the nineteenth-century tradition. (There is no need to emphasize here that the direction of this evolution would appear very different if instead of stopping at this point we thought of the transition from the nineteenth-century novel to the narrative diversity of our own period, with its recovery of allegory, romance, myth, vision . . .) All this being so, it will be understood why I approached the picaresque as a whole by setting it against the distant background of the realist novel[6] and looked at it mainly as the subsequent fortunes of a set of techniques to which the *Lazarillo* and the *Guzmán* had owed their artistic success and their historical uniqueness: those techniques which shaped the two novels in terms of the point of view of the *pícaro*-turned-writer.

I have hinted that in writing this book I did not start from any prior definition or taxonomy of point of view. Of course I was aware of the relevant bibliography, but was often disconcerted by its obsession with classification and its absolute disregard of chronology.[7] By chapter 3, however, I did have at my disposal certain sufficiently firm criteria on the subject: those I deduced from the analysis of the *Lazarillo* and the *Guzmán* (and those alone). The theory of point of view which I apply there consists, then, of a series of historical facts. This is the limitation – and for some, perhaps, the advantage – of my own point of view.

It was obvious, in fact, that there was no reason why an examination of how later novels used point of view as found in the *Lazarillo* and the *Guzmán* should take account of the possible merits of such novels in other respects. But it should be noted that they presented themselves quite clearly and deliberately as successors or rivals of our two masterpieces (as, of course, did the continuation by 'Mateo Luján de Sayavedra'): *The 'Pícara' Justina* announced as much right from the engraving on the title page;[8] the Buscón, in the very publisher's preliminaries, was called a 'rival of Guzmán de Alfarache' (p. 6); González's Guitón Honofre reasoned that 'since we have a first and a second *pícaro*, it is right to give them a companion' (see chapter 3, n. 71). The truth is that at the moment when the category *picaresque novel* was publicly established as a distinct entity it had less to do with the real-life *pícaro* than with the 'Pícaro' of Mateo Alemán. The *pícaro* of the picaresque novel was so decidedly a *literary* creation that it not only could be but positively had to be tested against the type of point of view elaborated in its models and the literary theory they implicitly contained.

I therefore considered it legitimate and consistent to pass over the virtues which a *different* approach might have revealed in the picaresque in the wake of the *Guzmán*, in favour of the historical argument I could demonstrate by subjecting it to such a test. Because at the very least, this comparison made it clear that after Mateo Alemán the picaresque, as a whole, did not continue in that direction which the pioneers of the genre had laid down and which constituted their true greatness. It did have some features which would later prove to coincide with features of the realist novel, certainly, but these were minor and merely anecdotal (character types or milieux, for example, but features which were never by any means inseparable from an appropriately distinctive narrative structure). On the contrary, by resorting, as it did, to imitating only the most superficial aspects of the *Lazarillo* and the *Guzmán*, it showed signs of a lack of inventiveness; in failing to create the character from that inner perspective which it claimed to be adopting, it was continuing – quite understandably – to cling to the same socio-literary prejudice which its predecessors had avoided with such rich results (and with such different attitudes, moreover). Nor did it seem to me that these negative features (not necessarily 'defects') – negative, that is, by reference to its models – were offset by any substantial positive features of a similar or comparable type. In particular, I did not find a fresh, different and meaningful use of point of view which might, as a substitute for the highly original use of it in the *Lazarillo* and the *Guzmán*, have allowed me fruitfully to pursue my line of enquiry.[9] I was quite sure of the merits of *The 'Pícara' Justina* and the *Buscón*, but I could not and cannot see them as being of the same order as those of the *Lazarillo* and the *Guzmán*, or occupying an equally original, relevant position in the history of prose fiction. So that I did not consider it necessary to attempt to explain them: that was a task for another, much more sophisticated book than this.

My only reason for indulging in all the foregoing truisms and repetitions is that I have the impression that certain statements in this book have occasionally been read without bearing in mind their context and their premises. I am thinking especially of the pages devoted to a commentary on *some* features of the *Buscón*. 'Libro genial . . . y pésima novela picaresca' ('A work of genius – and a very bad picaresque novel'), I called it (p. 75). This remark illustrates the problem well enough. Despite the somewhat epigrammatic turn of phrase (a bad epigram, unfortunately), I felt that the idea was clear enough from the context, and I even wondered whether in the final lines of the section 'His master's voice' I might have laboured the point somewhat monotonously. In short, what I said was that Quevedo's work can be called 'very bad' as a 'picaresque novel', if it is examined in terms of the range of elements which it openly *copies* from the *Lazarillo* and the *Guzmán*, at the beginning of the seventeenth century. I still consider that in order to refute this assessment of mine – without taking it out of context or misrepresenting it[10] – one would have to show that the quality of 'genius' which I also

attribute to the *Buscón* lies in its handling of the material derived
from the two earlier novels or the success with which it combines
this with other material.

For exponents of a certain type of critical appreciation, questions such as dating and sources – the sort of questions which
typify, to the point of caricature, a 'scholarly' approach – can
sometimes be of secondary interest; nevertheless, they often prove
actually to be *internal* factors in the text. The date of the *Buscón* is
an obvious case in point. In the action of the last chapter, the
death of the 'lidiador ahigadado' ('brave fighter'), Álvarez de
Soria, which occurred in late 1603 or early 1604, is presented as a
recent event (III, 10; p. 278); several more years must have passed
after this: at least enough for Pablos to have crossed to America,
found out that things go even 'worse' for him there (III, 10; p.
280), and write his memoirs. Well then, if, as everything indicates,
the *Buscón* was written and circulated around 1604,[11] it would
seem obvious that the story is not governed by any consistent
chronological arrangement; and if temporal consistency is not a
relevant criterion for Quevedo,[12] then it is frankly difficult to
suppose that Pablos is any more convincing or coherent in other
respects (and perhaps it is incompatible with the artistic
achievements which scholars of all critical tendencies would agree
in finding in our novel).

As long as the heyday of the picaresque novel lasted, it was as
inevitable for the reader to compare the *Buscón* with its main
narrative sources as it was imperative around 1604 for him to
check it against the most obvious chronological facts. Because
when a literary borrowing is explicit or self-evident, the author
himself is inviting us to compare the two texts in question. 'Critics
who give primacy to *Guzmán de Alfarache* in the formation of the
generic model [of the picaresque] will normally be ideological
critics. Reading *El Buscón* in *Guzmán*'s field of attraction brings
into prominence and evaluates features in it that could otherwise
be interpreted differently.' It should not be forgotten, however,
that the presence of the *Buscón* in this 'field of attraction' is not an
opinion, but a fact. The critic, whether ideological or otherwise,
can take account of it or ignore it (and in the latter case he can
speculate, for example, about how to interpret the picaresque

'with *Guzmán* put first and *Lazarillo* following').[13] But the literary historian – and this applies to me – cannot possibly disregard this reality.

The references to an archetype – whether this is used positively or negatively – are constituent dimensions of the text: one must perceive them and adjust one's instruments of observation accordingly. For a brief demonstration of this in the *Buscón*, we do not even need to look further than the section of the work I recalled a couple of paragraphs above, in connection with chronology. The two final chapters are, by virtue of their very position as well as their content, a hurriedly executed calque on the two versions of *Guzmán*. The first (III, 9), in which Pablos becomes an 'actor, poet and nuns' gallant', persistently reproduces incidents and situations from the continuation by 'Mateo Luján de Sayavedra' (II, 6, and especially III, 7–9);[14] the other (III, 10), though it contains traces of the apocryphal *Guzmán*, is much closer to the authentic version (II, iii, 6–7), in placing the protagonist, finally, in the underworld of Seville.

I will not labour the point that little of what Pablos does, says or writes in these two chapters can be reconciled with what we already know about him, and a number of things in them explicitly contradict it.[15] The question which occurs to me is of rather a different order: what is the point of so patent and insistent an imitation of books which were familiar to everyone? There is absolutely nothing to suggest that what we have here is a refutation, a parody or a radical reworking. Perhaps Quevedo's aim was that his readers should notice the coincidence of motifs and thereby appreciate all the better that he was outdoing (or attempting to outdo) his predecessors in witticisms and conceits? Nevertheless, these two chapters were clearly rather hastily put together: there is scarcely a trace in them of that careful, highly conscious elaboration which distinguishes Quevedo's art at its most characteristic (just consider the marvellously etched portrait of Cabra or the fantastic tableau of the 'grotesque' hidalgos). If the imitation was a challenge (the duel to be fought with different weapons), then Quevedo did not live up to his own example. And so? And so it seems all that is left is an ill-conceived, lifeless copy, whichever way you look at it, an almost entirely uncreative act of conformity with a highly successful genre, undertaken out of little more than a desire to follow fashion. Quevedo noticed that it was time for his novel to end (because even the division into three books and the approximate number of chapters in each were laid down in advance by the two versions of *Guzmán!*), and he hastily collected together a series of motifs from Alemán and 'Sayavedra' which he considered essential for the literary species to which the *Buscón* belonged to be identifiable. Quevedo's failure to provide inspiration and forms of his own – which even extends to such external details as the chapter division and is not compensated for by any really substantial original contributions – puts him on the same level as the author of the false *Guzmán*. At least in those sections which closely follow the models, then, such as the two chapters mentioned above, there is no reason to treat him with any more consideration than 'Sayavedra', or to spare him similar objections to those which Alemán levelled at his rival (see p. 38 above). An analysis of this sort, setting my own point of view within the dynamics (or the inertia) of history, is what lies behind my description of the *Buscón* as a 'very bad picaresque novel'.

That such a description is correct is confirmed particularly, it seems to me, by an admirable recent study.[16] There the issues I had raised in this little book, starting from the fundamental question 'why does Pablos write?', are taken up again one by one. Thus the 'radical inconsistency' to which I drew attention, between the shame of the *pícaro* as actor and the shamelessness of the *pícaro* as author, is reconsidered in that study, in an attempt to find a solution to it which might, in turn, take account of the fundamental question mentioned above. The solution offered there runs as follows: 'Pablos ridicules himself in order to avoid something he finds even more unbearable ... being ridiculed by others.' Needless to say, there is absolutely nothing in the text of the novel to suggest such an 'explanation'.[17] Where does it come from, then? From a very free interpretation of the 'Dedicatory Letter' which appears in two manuscripts of the *Buscón*, and, more specifically, of the phrase which claims that Pablos composes his memoirs 'in order that no one else should tell lies about his life (as has happened to others) ...'. Here again we are obviously dealing with a wholly gratuitous 'explanation'. Let us admit, however, that the 'Dedicatory Letter' seeks to justify in some way the fact that Pablos is writing his autobiography (see p. 75 above), and suppose for a moment that an adequate explanation could be deduced from it, even if this explanation were the very one I have just pointed out as being manifestly unacceptable. Even so, there is still one fact which it is absolutely essential to bear in mind: whether or not Quevedo actually wrote the 'Dedicatory Letter', it *did not form part of the first version of the work* (a first version which in no way differs from the second as regards the problems I am discussing at the moment).[18] It figures only in a couple of codices (those of Córdoba and Santander) and constitutes an addition separate from the original conception of the *Buscón*. Its intention, nevertheless, is clear: to justify in some way (I repeat) the existence of the *pícaro*'s memoirs. Nor is there any doubt that those five dull, hasty lines fail to provide the justification they claim – except in the most superficial, most emptily *pro forma* respect – or to resolve the other perplexities to which the novel gives rise when it is read in the light of the poetics of the *Lazarillo* and the *Guzmán*. But the fact that the 'Dedicatory Letter' does not achieve its objective is of only secondary importance here. Because its mere presence guarantees us that it *accepts* picaresque poetics – by now, alas, too late. Its author, whether this was Quevedo or an attentive reader (who, as we know, must have been a contemporary of his), noticed that the *Buscón* made use of a fair number of elements drawn from the *Lazarillo* and the *Guzmán*, but without giving them the profound coherence that these other works achieved thanks to their subtle handling of point of view, the masterly way in which they establish the continuity which exists between the *pícaro* as protagonist and the *pícaro* as writer. Therefore, being unable to remedy the incoherence within the text, where it was ineradicably ingrained, he endeavoured to attenuate it outside the text, by suggesting at least the vestige of an answer to the essential question 'why does Pablos write?'. Not only is the answer which the 'Dedicatory Letter' presents purely superficial, as we know, not only is it unable to prevent the book remaining a farrago of unconnected elements, but in addition it copies devices (badly) from the *Lazarillo* and the *Guzmán* (see pp.

76–7 above). It is a recantation, then, the admission of a mistake, and a vain attempt to mitigate it by returning to the sources which had been exploited in a shallow and inconsistent manner. The fact that an intelligent recent critic resorts to this shamefaced addition – as poor as it is revealing – notably confirms the impossibility of explaining why Pablos writes from within the novel itself.[19] On the contrary, the fact that it was felt necessary to add the 'Dedicatory Letter', with the models it reveals and the aims it has in view, endorses the legitimacy and appropriateness of reading Quevedo's novel in the light of the *Lazarillo* and the *Guzmán*, and shows that the modes of development in the *Buscón* are not in accordance with the picaresque premisses which it nevertheless adopts: in particular, that the autobiographical form 'neither constitutes a necessary corollary of the other elements of the book (character, plot, intention . . .) nor adds any meaning to them' (p. 73 above), but that it remains an 'empty shell', a slavish adherence to fashion.

In this way, then, history and criticism, in harmonious correlation with each other, combine to pass judgement on Quevedo's failure as a novelist. I do not think anyone should be offended by this statement. It is a failure which merely throws into sharper relief the magnitude of his success in *other* types of prose fiction (and in another, more mature stage of his career): in so splendid a 'moral fantasy' as *La hora de todos*, for example. Moreover, it is not so much a personal failure as the failure of a whole period. The fact is that my conclusions on the picaresque after the *Guzmán* are not at variance with those which have been reached for other European countries. 'In the period immediately after Cervantes – the period of Avellaneda, it would not be unfair to call it – the characteristics of French fiction in general are liveliness, persistence and ineffectiveness in equal proportions, each quality the inevitable counterpart of the others', while 'English fiction during the century was almost negligible'. One can never emphasize strongly enough the extent to which *Guzmán de Alfarache* and *Don Quixote* are the exception, and the rule lies in 'Luján de Sayavedra', the Quevedo of the *Buscón* or Avellaneda: in the dissipation of novelty into convention, 'towards confirming social, cultural orthodoxy'.[20]

Handbooks tend, in their accounts of the history of the European novel, to jump – over the void – from Cervantes to Defoe. Among the many careless, hasty features of this approach, the omission of Mateo Alemán is particularly serious (see n.5 above). All the same, we should have no compunction in admitting that neither the late Spanish picaresque nor the *roman comique* which mixes this up with the *Quixote* (along with so many other odds and ends) contributes very much to a history of fiction written with the perspective of the 'classical' realist novel in mind. There is something tragic in this disregard for the legacy of Cervantes and the best of the picaresque, at a time when the ink of *Guzmán de Alfarache* and the *Quixote* was not yet dry. Tragic because it was inevitable, not because it is incomprehensible. Or at least, I think my observations on the *Buscón* and the picaresque of 'the period of Avellaneda' help to make the fate of the novel in the rest of Europe comprehensible, as well as in Spain. I shall not be the one to undertake the task of explaining (to amplify the epigraph of my third chapter) why 'the novel slipped through the fingers of the whole of Europe' at the beginning of the seventeenth century. But this book does perhaps serve to indicate that no such explanation can be given without paying serious attention to the Spanish picaresque.

Notes

1 *Lazarillo de Tormes, or polysemy*

1 *De causis corruptarum artium*, I, ii, 6, in *Opera omnia*, ed. G. and J. A. Mayans, vol.VI (Valencia, 1785), p. 108.

2 Breaking with tradition, by identifying completely with pimps and prostitutes and portraying them with the same depth and seriousness as the noble protagonists, constitutes the most revolutionary feature of Fernando de Rojas's *Tragicomedia*: this is perhaps the fundamental thesis of María Rosa Lida de Malkiel's great work, *La originalidad artística de 'La Celestina'* (Buenos Aires, 1962; see also her posthumously published complementary study, 'El ambiente concreto en *La Celestina*', in *Estudios dedicados a J. H. Herriott*, Madison, Wisconsin, 1966, pp. 145–64), where the assertion I advance in the text here is amply confirmed. See n. 33 below, and chapter 3.

3 The Italianate *novella*, which was limited to a single situation and was incomparably less perceptive as regards the individuality and coherence of the protagonist's personality (when there was a protagonist), could obviously not serve as a model of how to give 'a complete account' of an 'individual', which is the avowed aim of the *Lazarillo*. This work is rich in comic folk tales (Marcel Bataillon was the first to study this successfully, in the important 'Introduction' to *La vie de Lazarillo de Tormès*, Paris, 1958), and its author knew and used the work of some *novelliere*; but the point is that it transcends this one-dimensional material by absorbing it into the plot, subordinating it to the progress of the action: jokes and anecdotes which previously were amusing only in themselves now also acquire new interest, as integral elements in the *Lazarillo*, from where they are placed, whom they happen to and how far they affect him. With regard to all this, see Fernando Lázaro Carreter, 'Construcción y sentido del *Lazarillo de Tormes*', *Ábaco*, I (Madrid, 1969), 45–134 [reprinted in his book, *'Lazarillo de Tormes' en la picaresca* (Barcelona, 1972), pp. 59–192]: a study of fundamental importance in every way, in which the subtle interplay of tradition and originality in the *Lazarillo* is examined with great insight.

4 A 'spoken epistle', as Claudio Guillén calls it in an essential article on 'La disposición temporal del *Lazarillo de Tormes*', *Hispanic Review*, 25 (1957), 268; and the adjective he uses is appropriate if it refers to the near-colloquial style. Guillén continues, on p. 271: 'The *Lazarillo* ... more than a mere story, is a *relación*, or report made by a man about himself'; this remark is corroborated by another, independent attempt to characterize this novel as a *carta relación* 'telle qu'on en reçoit des conquistadors et des découvreurs' (Charles V. Aubrun, in a course at the Sorbonne, 1953–4, a summary of which has been published in mimeograph by the FGEL, Paris, 1960, p. 1). [See now my

article 'Nuevos apuntes sobre la carta de Lázaro de Tormes', in *Homenaje a
Fernando Lázaro Carreter* (Madrid, 1983).]

5 The numbers in parentheses correspond, unless otherwise indicated, to
pages of the edition of the *Lazarillo* prepared by José Caso González (Madrid,
1967), whose exhaustive apparatus of variants makes it indispensable as the
text of reference. For those points where I have departed from this text,
mainly on the basis of the Burgos edition of 1554, and on all the other textual
problems of the *Lazarillo*, see my article 'En torno al texto crítico del *Lazarillo
de Tormes*', *Hispanic Review*, 38 (1970), 405–19 [and Alberto Blecua's essential
edition, Madrid, 1974 (Clasicos Castalia, 58)]. Italics within quotations are
mine throughout; I have modernized the orthography and a few other
details.

6 In another connection, Arturo Marasso noted the abuse of the syntagm 'you
write, sir, that I should write to you' ('escrebísme, señor, que os escriba') in
the very popular *Epístolas familiares* of Fray Antonio de Guevara (*Estudios de
literatura castellana*, Buenos Aires, 1955, p. 161): it is used no fewer than five
times, for instance, in the short Letter LX (ed. José M. de Cossío, vol. I,
Madrid, 1950, pp. 407–9).

7 It is defined thus by Angelo Poliziano, cited in Eugenio Garin, ed., *Prosatori
latini del Quattrocento* (Milan/Naples, 1952), p. xi, n. 3; [now in A. Poliziano,
Commento inedito alle 'Selve' di Stazio, ed. L. Cesarini Martinelli (Florence,
1978), p. 18. It is a quotation from Demetrius, *On Style*, 223.]

8 Compare, for example, Luis Vives, *De conscribendis epistolis*, VII, in *Opera omnia*,
vol. II, p. 293. See also n. 18 below.

9 Of the sort that now record births, marriages and deaths, for example. We
might add a dash of metaphysics to this list, with a quotation from Nicholas
of Cusa: '... ut nihil sit in universo, quod non gaudeat quadam singularitate,
quae in nullo alio reperibilis est' (cited by Eusebio Colomer, SJ, in the
collection *L'opera e il pensiero di Pico della Mirandola*, Florence, 1965, vol. II, p.
73); and with another from Gonzalo de Ayora: 'The subject of this work is not
universal man, nor the universality of causes, but man as an individual' (a
text discussed in J. A. Maravall, *Carlos V y el pensamiento político del
Renacimiento*, Madrid, 1960, p. 33).

10 *Renaissance Thought*, vol. II (New York, 1965), pp. 28 and 65; *Eight Philosophers
of the Italian Renaissance* (Stanford, 1966), p. 21. See also Joseph E. Gillet,
Torres Naharro and the Drama of the Renaissance, ed. Otis H. Green (Philadelphia, 1961), pp. 228–33 ('The discovery of man: letters'); José Carlos
Mainer, 'Notas a una nueva edición de la picaresca', *Ínsula*, 266 (January,
1969), p. 3d; [and n. 12 below].

11 In Garin, ed., *Prosatori Latini del Quattrocento*, p. xi, n. 3. The same
distinction is found in Vives's prologue to *De conscribendis epistolis*, p. 264, [and
in many other manuals on letter-writing; it comes from Cicero, *Epistulae*, II,
iv, 1.]

12 [See my 'Nuevos apuntes sobre la carta de Lázaro de Tormes'; I have
modified the rest of this paragraph, to being it into line with this article.]

13 See Fernando Lázaro Carreter, 'La ficción autobiográfica en el *Lazarillo de
Tormes*', in *Litterae Hispanae et Lusitanae* (Munich, 1966), pp. 195–213, [now
available in *'Lazarillo de Tormes' en la picaresca*, pp. 11–57]. Any reader
interested in the origins of first-person narrative form in the *Lazarillo* must

turn to this indispensable study, which examines the 'confluence of stimuli' that, as far as one can tell, seems to determine the course of the auto-biography: the need for verisimilitude, characteristic of humanism; the apparent influence of Apuleius and Lucian; and, especially, the pattern 'of the letter that follows the model "expetis me ... fortunae meae narrationem explicitam"' (p. 208), etc. My main concern here is not so much the possible source of the autobiographical device as its *a posteriori* meaning within the framework of the work in its finished form.

14 [Compare Antonio Vilanova, 'L'*Ane d'Or* d'Apulée, source et modèle du *Lazarillo de Tormes*', in Agustín Redondo, ed., *L'humanisme dans les lettres espagnoles* (Paris, 1979), pp. 267–85. Alberto Blecua, 'Libros de caballerías, latín macarrónico y novela picaresca: la adaptación castellana del *Baldus* (Sevilla, 1542)', *Boletín de la Real Academia de Buenas Letras de Barcelona*, 34 (1971–2), 147–239, has presented an interesting analogy to the auto-biography of Lazarillo, placing it significantly in the literary context out of which our novel also emerges.]

15 Here, as long as it is not taken as a hard and fast rule, is an interesting observation from one of the most distinguished novelists of the present day, Michel Butor, in *Essais sur le roman* (Paris, 1969), p. 75: 'Caractéristique à cet égard le fait que lors de toutes les mystifications romanesques, chaque fois que l'on a essayé de faire passer une fiction pour un document, prenons par exemple le *Robinson Crusoé* ou le *Journal de l'année de la peste* de Daniel Defoe, on a utilisé tout naturellement la première personne. En effet, si l'on avait pris la troisième, on aurait automatiquement provoqué la question: "Comment se fait-il que personne d'autre n'en sache rien?".'

16 More difficult to verify, but true at least *sub specie aeternitatis*, is the following shrewd observation on the author's anonymity from Américo Castro, *Hacia Cervantes*, second edition (Madrid, 1960), p. 137: 'Since a biography of such an insignificant character would have lacked all justification (the Roman-ticism of the nineteenth century was still a long way away), the author had to stay in the background and let the product of his imagination do the talking. The autobiographical style is thus shown to be inseparable from the very attempt to give artistic expression to a subject that was up to that time non-existent or despised... The use of autobiography in the *Lazarillo* is an inevitable corollary of its anonymity.' [For certain possible implications of the anonymity, see Francisco Rico, 'Para el prólogo del *Lazarillo*: "el deseo de alabanza"', in *Actes de la Table Ronde ... Picaresque Espagnole* (Montpellier, 1976), pp. 101–16. Compare postscript, n. 2 below.]

17 An aspect of the *Lazarillo* aptly emphasized by Eugenio Asensio, 'La peculiaridad literaria de los conversos', *Anuario de estudios medievales*, 4 (1967), 341, [reprinted in *La España imaginada de Américo Castro* (Barcelona, 1976), p. 104.]

18 'Esto fue el mesmo año que nuestro victorioso Emperador en esta insigne ciudad de Toledo entró y tuvo en ella Cortes, y se hicieron grandes regocijos y fiestas, como Vuestra Merced habrá oído. Pues en este tiempo estaba en mi prosperidad y en la cumbre de toda buena fortuna' ('This has been hap-pening in the same year that our victorious Emperor came to this illustrious city of Toledo and summoned the Cortes here, and great celebrations and festivities took place, as Your Worship has no doubt heard. Well at this time I

was prosperous and at the height of all good fortune', p. 145). So reads the final paragraph of the novel. The use of the past tenses ('fue', 'estaba') may seem surprising. From Lázaro's wedding to the moment when His Worship becomes interested in 'the case', some time has elapsed ('siempre en el año le da...'; 'every year he gives her...', etc., p. 143). But I think 'fue' and 'estaba' refer not to the (more or less) distant past of the wedding, but to the present time of 'the case' and of the (ostensible) composition of the novel. What I believe we have here is a learned syntactic formula, an imitation of the 'epistolary past' commonly used in Latin ('Une tendance existe dans la correspondance à se placer du point de vue du destinataire lisant la lettre et, par suite, à exprimer au passé ce qui est présent pour l'expéditeur', A. Ernout and F. Thomas, *Syntaxe latine*, second edition, Paris, 1959, p. 227). If I am right, the use of the 'epistolary past' applied to present events would underline the fact that the *Lazarillo* is disguised as a letter, and would give the final paragraph an ironic tone similar to the one in the Prologue, where the lowly subject matter of the novel is dressed up in classical citations and topoi from the noble tradition. Marasso, *Estudios de literatura castellana*, p. 159, suggests that the passage in question should be seen as containing a parodic echo of the end of the *Georgics* (IV, 559: 'Haec ... canebam ..., Caesar dum magnus...'); this may be so (compare Lázaro Carreter, 'Construcción y sentido', pp. 118–19); but in any case, it should be pointed out that Virgil's 'canebam' corresponds exactly to the 'scribebam' with which Cicero dates a letter (for example, *Ad Atticum*, IV, iii, 5) or to the 'dictabam' with which Horace indicates where he has just finished composing an *epistula* (I, x, 49). [An appropriate parallel can also be found in an autobiography such as the *Res Gestae* of Augustus (IV, 4; XXXV, 2, etc.); in Spanish one has only to compare the final strophe of the *Cristopathía* of Juan de Quirós, published precisely in Toledo and in 1552: 'Quando el autor en este estilo llano / la gran passión de Cristo celebrava, / Máximo Carlo, Emperador Romano, / sobre el Danubio en armas fulminaba, / quando a Germania su derecha mano / y a la dureza del saxón domaba, / testigo el Albis de su gran victoria, / que por los siglos quedará en memoria' (p. 153). See Rico, 'Nuevos apuntes sobre la carta de Lázaro de Tormes', n. 45.]

19 It seems obvious that the Archpriest is the only point of contact between Lázaro and His Worship: it is not surprising, then, that the third character in 'the case', the town crier's wife (as we shall see), is similarly the main point of contact (to put it delicately) between the two servants of His Worship. The 'case' that interests His Worship is, in the final analysis, the key to his own relationship with Lázaro.

20 This is one of the most important conclusions of Claudio Guillén's splendid essay 'La disposición temporal del *Lazarillo de Tormes*'. Guillén hesitates over the identification of 'the case', pp. 269–70: 'Could the Archpriest of San Salvador's friend have known about the disgraceful relationship between the latter and Lázaro? ... Is Lázaro's final confession an answer to a demand for him to account for himself, or not?'; but I believe that the passage in the Prologue (p. 62) which I have cited several times and its analogue in the final chapter (p. 144), both explicitly mentioning 'the case', put the question beyond doubt: they give us the 'argument', the efficient and final causes (as a Scholastic would say) of the *Lazarillo*. In addition, Guillén presents the town

crier's letter as 'an act of obedience' (p. 268); however, he does not relate the novelistic construction, in the strict sense, to this act: rather, following Bergson (see Lázaro Carreter, 'Construcción y sentido', p. 55, n.), he insists that 'the climactic points of the work coincide with a series of facts of consciousness: with the essential components of Lázaro's memory' (p. 271). This is true; but neither these 'facts of consciousness' nor the town crier's memory are presented as determining causes of the book's composition (on the other hand this is largely what happens in *Guzmán de Alfarache*). I do not make these observations (which are subject to correction) in order to follow the niggardly custom of pointing out a coincidence between oneself and X and immediately adding: 'But X fails to notice...'. I simply wish to indicate that Guillén's approach and my own are both different and complementary, and for this reason both produce a fairly convincing interpretation of the *Lazarillo* (compare Guillén's initial comments, p. 264). [The identification of 'the case' with the *ménage à trois* of the final chapter, on the one hand, and, on the other hand, the (partial) explanation of the *Lazarillo* as a response to the question formulated by His Worship precisely and exclusively with reference to such a 'case' (and even the use of this term in discussing the novel), have become generally accepted on the basis of the first section of my article 'Problemas del *Lazarillo*', *Boletín de la Real Academia Española*, 46 (1966), 277–87, thanks especially to the acceptance of my hypothesis by Fernando Lázaro Carreter in 'Construcción y sentido'. But one cannot interpret the novel solely on the basis of 'the case' (far from it!), nor has the latter always been discussed with the necessary critical rigour in recent works on the subject: among the latest contributions, see the useful *mise au point* by Víctor García de la Concha, *Nueva lectura del 'Lazarillo'* (Madrid, 1981), pp. 15–91; the stimulating suggestions of G. A. Shipley, 'The critic as witness for the prosecution: making the case against Lázaro de Tormes', *PMLA*, 97 (1982), 179–94; and my observations in the article 'Nuevos apuntes sobre la carta de Lázaro de Tormes'.]

21 Compare most recently Lázaro Carreter, 'Construcción y sentido', p. 80 (and *passim* for the other symmetries and contrasts that reinforce the structure of the novel: I am concerned only with a few points which are especially relevant to my central theme). [There are some useful observations in Margit Frenk, 'Tiempo y narrador en el *Lazarillo* (Episodio del ciego)', *Nueva revista de filología hispánica*, 24 (1975), 197–218.]

22 'And he broke my teeth, which I have been without ever since, *right up till now*' ('Y me quebró los dientes, sin los cuales *hasta hoy día* me quedé', p. 73). Here again Lázaro turns the reader's attention to the moment at which he is writing: that 'hoy día' is 'el día de hoy' ('today', p. 141) when Lázaro says he is in His Worship's service, 'el día de hoy' (p. 144) when he is relating 'the case' to him.

23 A fact perceptively pointed out in Lázaro Carreter, 'Construcción y sentido', p. 68. [For the exact sense of the comment in question, see the appendix to Francisco Rico, ed., *Lazarillo de Tormes* (Barcelona, 1980) (Clásicos Universales Planeta, 6), pp. 106–9; the volume is a corrected and augmented reprint of the introduction and edition contained in *La novela picaresca española*, vol. 1 (Barcelona, 1967 [1966]).]

24 In *Théorie de la littérature. Textes des formalistes russes*, ed. T. Todorov (Paris, 1965), p. 184.

25 Shrewdly studied recently by Elias L. Rivers, 'Para la sintaxis del soneto', in *Studia philologica. Homenaje ofrecido a Dámaso Alonso*, vol. III (Madrid, 1963), pp. 228–9.

26 One has only to refer to *Seis calas en la expresión literaria española*, second edition (Madrid, 1956), in collaboration with Carlos Bousoño, [and more recently *Pluralità e correlazione in poesia* (Bari, 1971).]

27 Attention is drawn to what was said in n. 21 above.

28 The anonymous author's contemporaries must have been very much alive to the way in which the multiple novelistic elements converge towards the singular 'case'. The edition of the *Lazarillo* printed by Salcedo in Alcalá de Henares, also in 1554, contains various interpolations added to the original text. Now the first extra passage in the Alcalá edition has no other object than to aim additional arrows, as it were, in the form of prophecies, at the same target of chapter 7: Lázaro, who in Escalona does not understand why the rope should be 'such bad food that it chokes you without you eating it' (p. 147), nor why the horns should give him 'an unpalatable meal' (p. 148), finds the answer to such perplexing questions on the day he lends his services as town crier to hang a 'thief from Toledo' (p. 142, n. 10), and the nights he spends waiting up for his wife 'until dawn' (p. 143, n. 23). The interpolator has underlined the point rather heavy-handedly, but he has admirably perceived the design of the work.

29 'As God is my witness, *nowadays*, whenever I come across someone of that ilk [another squire], with that pompous walk and bearing, I pity him, at the thought that he might be suffering what I saw the other one suffer . . . I was only unhappy with him on one point: I wished he were not so proud, and that he would abandon a little of his pretentiousness considering how great his need was' (pp. 115–16).

30 Again the Alcalá interpolator grasps the meaning of the chapter well: when Lázaro discovers the very understandable reasons behind a certain false miracle, the pardoner, he says, 'put his finger to his mouth, indicating that I should keep quiet. I did so because it suited me...' (p. 151).

31 See Eugenio Asensio, *Itinerario del entremés* (Madrid, 1965), p. 208.

32 E. Panofsky, 'Albrecht Dürer and classical antiquity', in *Meaning in the Visual Arts* (Garden City, NY, 1955), p. 278; compare, by the same author, *Renaissance and Renascenses in Western Art* (Copenhagen, 1960), pp. 118 ff. [Now M. Dalai Emiliani, ed., *La prospettiva rinascimentale: codificazioni e trasgressioni* (Florence, 1979–80) contains an exhaustive bibliography.]

33 On one essential point, nevertheless, the author would seem to be following literary convention: in portraying the lowly characters in a comic manner at times (see Lida de Malkiel, *La originalidad artística de 'La Celestina'*, p. 609), and putting the emphasis in his picture of the protagonist on a humorous feature, the circumstances of the final 'case'. However, I think that what is involved here is not so much a humorous caricature of the low-class characters, inspired by the old theories about the relationship between style and social class (which were invariably followed in the theatre of the time, for example), as the results of an ironic and destructive view of the whole of society – one has only to consider the ridiculous role allotted to 'señor don

Fulano' ('Sir So and So') in the Prologue, (p. 62). The author, of course, does not take Lázaro completely seriously; but neither does he take seriously 'those who inherited noble estates' (p. 62).

34 'The narrator is a grown man, formed, mature, enlightened. Lázaro, rather than Lazarillo, is the work's centre of gravity'; this important observation by Claudio Guillén, in 'La disposición temporal del *Lazarillo de Tormes*', p. 271, should always be borne in mind.

35 Joseph E. Gillet, *Propalladia and Other Works of Bartolomé de Torres Naharro*, vol. I (Bryn Mawr, 1943), p. 143; see also vol. IV, *Torres Naharro and the Drama of the Renaissance*, pp. 440–1 [and, if one wishes to pursue the parallel between Renaissance painting and literature, the interesting article by A. M. Lecoq, '*Finxit*. Le peintre comme *fictor* au XVIe siècle', *Bibliothèque d'Humanisme et Renaissance*, 37 (1975), 225–43.] Marcel Bataillon has convincingly demonstrated the Spanish Erasmians' distaste for fiction, and their 'ideal of truthful and improving literature' (*Erasmo y España*, translated by A. Alatorre, second edition, Mexico, 1966, p. 627; original title *Érasme et l'Espagne*, Paris, 1937); this is precisely the reason why I have chosen a couple of quotations, from Torres Naharro and Salutati, which cannot possibly contain any trace of Erasmianism.

36 'Verisimilitudo ... media est fabulosae fictionis et certissimae veritatis', C. Salutati, *Epistolario*, ed. F. Novati, vol. IV (Rome, 1905), p. 125. A comparable conception of linguistic *verisimilitudo* is precisely what inspires the language of the *Lazarillo*: compare Rico, ed., *La novela picaresca española*, vol. I, pp. lxvii–lxxii.

37 See for example E. C. Riley, *Cervantes's Theory of the Novel* (Oxford, 1962), pp. 163–78 [and more recently the vast undertaking by Antonio García Berrio, *Formación de la teoría literaria moderna* (Madrid/Murcia, 1977–80)].

38 This is not a spy story where people hide a cyanide pill in their mouth as a last resort: in ancient times, the mouth often functioned as a purse (see A. Rumeau's perceptive study, 'Notes au *Lazarillo*: lanzar', *Bulletin hispanique*, 64 (1962), 233–5); rings were kept in it in *La lozana andaluza*, ed. A. Vilanova (Barcelona, 1952), pp. 17 and 28, etc.

39 'My mouth, which *must have been* open ...', 'he believed *no doubt* that it was the serpent whistling, and so it *must have* seemed', 'in the way it *must have* been', 'he *must have* said ...' (pp. 97–8).

40 It is certainly not surprising that this passage has attracted the interest of Spanish critics commenting on the radical subjectivism of the *nouveau roman*: see José M. Castellet, *La hora del lector* (Barcelona, 1957), pp. 123–4.

41 Buying in bulk was the mark of a great noble household; on this and other features of the portrait of the squire, as pointed out both by the squire himself and by Lázaro, see the second part of my article, 'Problemas del *Lazarillo*', pp. 288–96 [and the discussion of various points in Harry Sieber, *Language and Society in 'La vida de Lazarillo de Tormes'* (Baltimore, 1978), pp. 31–44, and Agustín Redondo, 'Historia y literatura: el personaje del escudero de *El Lazarillo*', in *La picaresca ... Actas del primer congreso internacional ...* (Madrid, 1979), pp. 421–35].

42 This is not the place to examine the skilful use of verbal tenses and persons, the means by which the passage creates a sense of immediacy, and so on. [For several interesting points, see Domingo Ynduráin, 'Algunas notas sobre el

"tractado tercero" del *Lazarillo de Tormes*', in *Studia hispanica in honorem R. Lapesa*, vol. III (Madrid, 1975), pp. 507–17.]

43 These eternal questions attracted considerable attention at the time of the *Lazarillo* (see the impressive work by Ernst Cassirer, *Das Erkenntnisproblem in der Philosophie und Wissenschaft der neueren Zeit*, Berlin, 1906), but one should not necessarily assume that they concerned the anonymous author in the abstract, as a philosophical problem: I would argue, however, that they undoubtedly interested him as points of reference in the evaluation of individual behaviour and social praxis.

44 Of course this remark cannot be taken to apply in all cases, as Alain Robbe-Grillet seems to claim in *Pour un nouveau roman* (Paris, 1963), p. 37: need one look further than Cervantes?

45 Several critics have pointed out a clear tendency to personify objects in the *Lazarillo*; see most recently Claudio Guillén, ed., '*Lazarillo de Tormes*' and '*El Abencerraje*' (New York, 1966), pp. 16–17, [and A. D. Deyermond, '*Lazarillo de Tormes*'. *A Critical Guide* (London, 1975)].

46 'Presentación ilusionista', as María Rosa Lida de Malkiel aptly terms it in 'Función del cuento popular en el *Lazarillo de Tormes*', in *Actas del primer congreso internacional de hispanistas* (Oxford, 1964), p. 356, [an article now reprinted in her book, *El cuento popular y otros ensayos* (Buenos Aires, 1976), pp. 107–22].

47 Compare Frank Durand's very good essay 'The author and Lázaro: levels of comic meaning', *Bulletin of Hispanic Studies*, 45 (1968), 100–1.

48 If Lázaro were a traditional folk character (as has been conjectured, in my opinion against the available evidence), and everyone knew the outcome of his adventures, then we would be dealing here with a technique similar to that of *El Caballero de Olmedo*, where Lope de Vega deliberately includes a whole series of allusions to the denouement in order to create superb dramatic tension; see my article, '*El Caballero de Olmedo*: amor, muerte, ironía', *Papeles de Son Armadans*, no. 139 (October, 1967), 38–56; [a revised version of this essay can be found in the prologue to my third edition of Lope's play (Madrid, 1981). The leading specialist in the field, Maxime Chevalier, 'Des contes au roman: l'éducation de Lazarille', *Bulletin hispanique*, 81 (1979), 189–99, is now inclined to play down the importance of the contribution of elements from folklore to the formation of the novel and completely rules out the idea that Lazarillo was a traditional character].

49 José Ortega y Gasset, *Obras completas*, second edition, vol. III (Madrid, 1950), p. 199.

50 See also Guillén, ed. '*Lazarillo de Tormes*' and '*El Abencerraje*' pp. 24–7, which contains a number of pertinent comments.

51 Compare Bruce W. Wardropper, 'El trastorno de la moral en el *Lazarillo*', *Nueva revista de filología hispánica*, 15 (1961), 441–2; *La novela picaresca española*, vol. I, p. 14, n. 27; Francisco Márquez Villanueva, *Espiritualidad y literatura en el siglo XVI* (Madrid, 1968), pp. 92–9 (Professor Márquez discusses the subject in a lengthy study, 'La actitud espiritual del *Lazarillo de Tormes*', pp. 69–137, which is of prime importance for anyone interested in the problems of this novel); [R. W. Truman, 'Lázaro de Tormes and the *homo novus* tradition', *Modern Language Review*, 64 (1969), 62–7, and '*Lazarillo de Tormes*, Petrarch's *De remediis adversae fortunae*, and Erasmus's *Praise of Folly*', *Bulletin of Hispanic Studies*, 52 (1975), 33–53].

52 See Manuel García Pelayo, *El reino de Dios, arquetipo político* (Madrid, 1959); Francisco Rico, *El pequeño mundo del hombre. Varia fortuna de una idea en las letras españolas* (Madrid, 1970), pp. 107–17 ('De política').

53 *Obras de don Juan Manuel*, ed. J. M. Castro y Calvo and M. de Riquer, vol. I (Barcelona, 1955), p. 41, [or, preferably, in J. M. Blecua, ed., Don Juan Manuel, *Obras completas*, vol. I (Madrid, 1982), p. 78].

54 J. de Santa María, *Tratado de república y policía cristiana* (Valencia, 1619), fol. 60.

55 P. Mexía, *Silva de varia lección*, II, 36 (ed. Madrid, 1669, p. 276).

56 A text cited and commented on in Hans Baron, *The Crisis of the Early Italian Renaissance* (Princeton, 1966), pp. 419 and 556, n. 21; see in general pp. 418–24. I have chosen this text out of an enormous range of similar ones, because it contains an allusion to the possibility of making a career in administration and indicates that this is open to anyone; it should be noted that Lázaro aspires to an 'office under the crown' (to become a 'civil servant', as we would say nowadays).

57 See Eugenio Garin, *L'umanesimo italiano* (Bari, 1965), p. 58 (compare pp. 76–8, 104, etc.). A vast amount has been written on the subject: for example, one can consult José Antonio Maravall, *El mundo social de 'La Celestina'* (Madrid, 1964), pp. 84–111 [and 'La aspiración social de "medro" en la novela picaresca', *Cuadernos hispanoamericanos*, 312 (June, 1976), 590–625; Enrique Tierno Galván, *Sobre la novela picaresca y otros escritos* (Madrid, 1974), pp. 11–114, to cite just three studies whose broad perspective is particularly fruitful in relation to the *Lazarillo*].

58 As Antonio de Torquemada summarizes it in the *Coloquios satíricos* (1553), which can be found in the *Nueva biblioteca de autores españoles*, vol. VII (Madrid, 1907), p. 542; the sixth *Coloquio*, from which the passage cited here is taken, offers many relevant points of comparison with the *Lazarillo* (see *La novela picaresca española*, vol. I, pp. liii, 6, and 59; Lázaro Carreter, 'Construcción y sentido', pp. 125–7: the problem was undoubtedly a highly topical one at that time.

59 In the opinion of contemporaries this was 'the most contemptible position there is' (Marcel Bataillon drew attention to this: see references in *La novela picaresca española*, vol. I, p. 77; Márquez Villanueva, 'La actitud espiritual del *Lazarillo de Tormes*' p. 105, n. 64; [and especially M. J. Woods, 'Pitfalls for the moralizer in *Lazarillo de Tormes*', *Modern Language Review*, 74 (1979), 580–98, which contains further interesting information – on clerics' concubines, etc. – which serves to situate 'the case' in the social context of the mid-sixteenth century].

60 Note that the conclusion stills holds good even if we take 'virtue' to mean the Machiavellian *virtù*, [almost in the sense of the 'effort and cunning' that Lázaro praises in the Prologue; see my 'Para el prólogo del *Lazarillo*', pp. 103–4 and n. 6]. Carlos P. Otero has announced he is preparing an article on the 'Alegría y virtud de Lázaro', which will doubtless throw useful light on the subject.

61 For Wardropper, 'the entire book is an attempt to investigate the social and personal consequences of a perverse morality' ('El trastorno de la moral en el *Lazarillo*, p. 444). Compare also R. L. Colie, *Paradoxia Epidemica. The Renaissance Tradition of Paradox* (Princeton, 1966), p. 296, although from the

context it is not clear whether she has understood the *Lazarillo*. [In an article published in 1971, and now included with some additions in his book *Erasmo y el erasmismo* (Barcelona, 1977), 'Un problema de influencia de Erasmo en España. *El Elogio de la locura*', pp. 327–46, Marcel Bataillon suggests the possibility that the *Lazarillo* may have been subtly inspired by the *Moria* of Erasmus 'in that the story is told by a *stultus* who is satisfied with his *stultitia* and proud of raising himself, as he does, to social and literary dignity'. In the light of W. Kaiser, *Praisers of Folly: Erasmus, Rabelais, Shakespeare* (Cambridge, Mass., 1963), pp. 35–50 (a work with which I was not acquainted when I wrote the present chapter), one might suppose that my reading of the *Lazarillo* has the effect of establishing some connection between it and the *Moria*. But the probable relationship of our novel to the tradition of the 'paradoxical encomium' is particularly complex and intriguing: the very anonymity of the book might enter into a discussion of the subject (see n. 45 in my 'Nuevos apuntes sobre la carta de Lázaro de Tormes').]

62 Introduction to *La vie de Lazarillo*, p. 52.

63 The first time I read these pages in public (in a very beautiful place in New England), a good-natured lady in the audience immediately showed signs of disapproval at this point; and during the discussion which followed she announced that she did not find the episode remotely amusing.

64 Marcel Bataillon, *Défense et illustration du sens littéral*, The Presidential Address of the Modern Humanities Research Association (Leeds, 1967), p. 24: a work I would warmly recommend to the reader.

65 See for example my 'Problemas del *Lazarillo*', p. 277, etc., and vol. 1, pp. l and lxxi; several studies which have appeared almost simultaneously have arrived independently at similar conclusions: besides the edition of the *Lazarillo* by Claudio Guillén, pp. 26–7, and the study by Frank Durand, 'The author and Lázaro', one should consult the extremely ingenious article by Stephen Gilman on 'The death of Lazarillo de Tormes', *PMLA*, 81 (1966), 149–66, [or now, among others, R. W. Truman, 'Parody and irony in the self-portrayal of Lázaro de Tormes', *Modern Language Review*, 63 (1968), 600–5, and H. Mancing, 'The deceptiveness of *Lazarillo de Tormes*', *PMLA*, 90 (1975), 426–32, although these studies are not always concerned with reconciling the ironic features that are brought out in the work and the 'tragic' interpretation of the *Lazarillo* which is offered quite separately from them].

66 There is just one point in the work, Lazarillo's commentary on the squire's deceptively fine bearing, when an explanatory statement in terms of an absolute seems to be made: 'Oh Lord, how many of these people must Thou have, scattered throughout the world, who suffer for this wretched thing they call honour what they will not suffer for Thee' (p. 110). The references to God placed in the mouth of the town crier are frequently ironic ('God' is the one who enlightens him and leads him to the Archpriest, 'God' the one who provides him with a 'thousand blessings', the priest's concubine, etc.), and are always open to the suspicion that they might refer to as conventional an idea of God as the one invoked by the pardoner during the false miracle (see Gilman, 'The death of Lazarillo de Tormes', pp. 155–8 [and more recently the pertinent observations advanced in V. G. de la Concha, 'La intención religiosa del *Lazarillo*', *Revista de filología española*, 55 (1972), 243–77]). But I think that the passage cited at the beginning of this note is presented just as

seriously as the same idea is expressed by various thoughtful, serious contemporary authors (see *La novela picaresca española*, vol. I, pp. liii-v). Now such a contrast with the absolutes of religious belief is not expressed again anywhere else (and it is rather out of character coming from the young Lazarillo). For this reason, I would guess that the author was not simply aiming to present to us a picture of a world which has made everything relative because it has forgotten the true God: if that had been his aim, he would have done so, as he does in this passage. On the contrary, this odd unequivocal allusion seems to confirm that the total ambiguity of the work as a whole is quite deliberate. In principle, it is unsound to assume that an author was an unbeliever around 1550 without very solid positive proof – for a good presentation of a variety of material relevant to this note, see O. H. Green, *Spain and the Western Tradition*, vol. III (Madison and Milwaukee, 1965), pp. 180–8, 301–6, [Julio Caro Baroja, *Las formas complejas de la vida religiosa. Religión, sociedad y carácter en la España de los siglos XVI y XVII* (Madrid, 1978), pp. 197–207 and *passim*, and Joseph Pérez, 'La unidad religiosa en la España del siglo XVI', in *Seis lecciones sobre la España de los Siglos de Oro. Homenaje a M. Bataillon* (Seville/Bordeaux, 1981), pp. 95–110]. This consideration, and the conviction that Lázaro's words cited above cannot be taken ironically, lead me to imagine the author as one of the many sincere believers of the time who found no difficulty in separating reason and faith: like one of the nominalists who were the dominant faction in the University of Alcalá, or Salamanca, where Gómez Pereira was educated: that aggressive, suspicious figure whose *Antoniana Margarita* came out at the same time as the *Lazarillo* – see Bataillon, *Erasmo y España*, pp. 16–18; [M. Andrés, *La teología española en el siglo XVI*, vol. II (Madrid, 1976), pp. 78–81 and *s.v.*; Vicente Muñoz Delgado, *Lógica, ciencia y humanismo en la renovación teológica de Vitoria y Cano* (Madrid, 1980);]like a kindred spirit of the sceptic Francisco Sánchez, who in his *Quod nihil scitur* (completed in 1576) denied the possibility of attaining any truth except of a personal, momentary kind, and left the certainty of faith out of the argument entirely, without using it to solve the problem of knowledge (*Opera medica et philosophica*, Toulouse, 1636, p. 813). As is well known, the situation was an old one (even older than the Averroist double truth), and it would almost be true to say that it had been responsible for creating the habit of making a distinction, in the examination of a whole range of questions, between natural truths, of a secular nature, and supernatural truths, of a religious nature; compare, for example, the valuable monograph by O. H. Green, 'Sobre las dos Fortunas', in *Studia philologica. Homenaje ofrecido a Dámaso Alonso*, vol. II (Madrid, 1960), pp. 143–54, [and Paul Oskar Kristeller, *Renaissance Thought and its Sources* (New York, 1979), pp. 196–209].

67 'Saber la verdad segura, y presto.' See the excellent study by Juan Bautista Avalle-Arce, 'Conocimiento y vida en Cervantes', *Filología*, 5 (1959), 1–34, now available in his *Deslindes cervantinos* (Madrid, 1961), pp. 15–80, [and *Nuevos deslindes cervantinos* (Barcelona, 1975), pp. 15–72].

2 The life and opinions of Guzmán de Alfarache

1 *Discursos* ('discourses') was the term used to translate the title of Montaigne's work in the seventeenth century (see J. Marichal, *La voluntad de estilo*, Barcelona, 1957, pp. 122, 128–9), and it was also what Ambrosio de Morales

called the fifteen exquisite essays (now forgotten, alas) which he interpolated into *Las obras del maestro Fernán Pérez de Oliva* (Córdoba, 1586). A
number of other examples could be cited; suffice it here to point out that
Alemán himself frequently uses the term.

2 *Lección y sentido del 'Guzmán de Alfarache'* (Madrid, 1948) (there is a good
summary, by the author himself, in *Nosotros y nuestros clásicos*, second edition,
Madrid, 1968, pp. 125–30). Although we do not entirely agree on various
points, on a number of others my approach is based on that of Professor
Moreno Báez and accepts his conclusions. I should like to refine here upon
what I wrote in *La novela picaresca española*, vol. I, pp. cxliii–cxliv: I now
consider that it is indeed legitimate to see 'the central thesis of the novel
[as] the possibility that the most wretched of men may be saved', together
with the series of themes related to this notion (*Lección y sentido*, pp. 84–5);
but 'central' not so much because the author emphasizes it in theoretical
terms – he devotes more explicit attention to other matters and aims to
educate the reader on '*every kind* of vice' (II, prologue; p. 467) – but rather
because of what it signifies in Guzmán's life; 'central', then, as a *novelistic
factor.*

3 Especially in the second part, as Donald McGrady notes in his very useful
Mateo Alemán (New York, 1968), p. 69. It seems clear to me that this is due
to that same desire to counteract oversimplifications on the part of common
people (already anticipated in the prologue to the first part, p. 92) which
led Alemán to take great care that the frontispiece of the second part bore
the complete title (which is explained, moreover, in the text, II, i, 6; p. 546,
and the preliminaries, p. 467). Furthermore it is undeniable that the
didactic aim is crystallized in 'digressions' right from the very outset (one
need look no further than the opening chapter, where the discursive
element already occupies appreciably more space than the narrative), even
if Alemán needed a few trial runs before he hit on the definitive formulae (it
is significant in this connection that the long invective against scriveners at
the beginning should be delivered by a 'learned preacher', I, i, 1; p. 116).

4 I have used the text of *Guzmán de Alfarache* published in *La novela picaresca
española*, vol. I, first edition, to which page numbers refer. In the introduction to this volume, pp. lxxvii–clxxxiii, a number of points which I merely
state here are developed and documented. [There is a second edition
(Barcelona, 1970), in which I was able to include some complementary
bibliographical information and several additional notes, but was not able
to correct the proofs (as I pointed out on p. cxci and in other publications of
mine); as the revision carried out by the publishers was very defective, this
text contains a great many misprints, some of which are serious and which
have unfortunately been copied by subsequent editors. Now available in a
separate volume (Barcelona, 1983) are a reprint of the text (with the
pagination unchanged) and of part of the introduction, together with some
complementary material and a thematic index.]

5 As has been noted simultaneously and independently in *La novela picaresca
española*, vol. I, p. cxv, and 'Estructuras y reflejos de estructuras en el
Guzmán de Alfarache', *Modern Language Notes*, 82 (1967), 183–4; and in
Edmond Cros's valuable *thèse*, *Protée et le gueux. Recherches sur les origines et la
nature du récit picaresque dans 'Guzmán de Alfarache'* (Paris, 1967), pp. 118–28,

etc. I have not seen F. Mäurer-Rothenberger, *Die Mitteilungen des 'Guzmán de Alfarache'* (Berlin, 1967).

6 'An author's worldview is a poetic construct, something he himself has created, not only when he pretends to adopt one that is not his own, but when he has absolutely no desire to pretend, and lets the worldview he himself lives out in his day-to-day life gradually take shape, for to fashion and perfect it, to the point that it becomes something exemplary, constitutes poetic creation', Amado Alonso, *Materia y forma en poesía*, second edition (Madrid, 1960), pp. 78–9.

7 [See simply Rico, *El pequeño mundo del hombre*, pp. 128–51, and '*Laudes litterarum*: humanisme et dignité de l'homme dans l'Espagne de la Renaissance', in Agustín Redondo, ed., *L'humanisme dans les lettres espagnoles* (Paris, 1979), pp. 31–50. Michel Cavillac, 'Mateo Alemán et la modernité', *Bulletin hispanique*, 82 (1980), 380–401, now insists that 'in the *Guzmán* pessimism is a polemical modality of the character's discourse', 'the point of view of the *pícaro'*.]

8 And thus gains his freedom, by denouncing a conspiracy. Of course, this contradicts the initial 'Declaration' (p. 96, quoted in the text) and the numerous allusions in the main body of the text to the miseries Guzmán suffered in the galley while writing his autobiography. Alemán frees his character only in order to leave the way open for a third part, in which Guzmán was to lead a uniformly virtuous life, [as is substantially the case in the mediocre continuation of the novel by Félix Machado de Silva; see A. San Miguel, '*Tercera parte del Guzmán de Alfarache*. La promesa de Alemán y su cumplimiento por el portugués Machado de Silva', *Iberoromania*, 1 (1974), 95–120]. In fact, the fundamental point was that Guzmán should write the book after having become a definitively reformed character (and having achieved justification: see Moreno Báez, *Lección y sentido*, p. 70 and n. 75, and my edition, p. 900, n. 12), firmly established in a particular point of view: whether he wrote it in the galleys or elsewhere did not greatly matter. For structural purposes, however, the work must be read as if it had been composed in the galley: Guzmán's liberation is something added at the last moment and affects only the last few lines.

9 This thesis is advanced by A. del Monte, *Itinerario del romanzo picaresco spagnolo* (Florence, 1957), pp. 72–3, among others.

10 '*Honra*, that is … external respectability based on dress, way of life, inherited social position', a perfect definition from Marcel Bataillon, 'Les nouveaux chrétiens dans l'essor du roman picaresque', *Neophilologus*, 48 (1964), 283; see also, by the same author, 'L'honneur et la matière picaresque', *Annuaire du Collège de France*, 63 (1963), 485–90, [studies which, like that mentioned in the next note, are now available in Spanish in Marcel Bataillon, *Pícaros y picaresca, 'La pícara Justina'* (Madrid, 1969)].

11 See Marcel Bataillon, '"La picaresca". À propos de *La pícara Justina*', in *Wort und Text. Festschrift für Fritz Schalk* (Frankfurt am Main, 1963), pp. 234–9; Rico, *La novela picaresca española*, vol. I, pp. cxxii–cxxv, 260.

12 'Truly I must confess to my competitor … that his discourses are such that I envy him and wish they were mine. But allow me to say the same as those who say that if on another occasion apart from this he should wish to use them, they would be works so honourable to him …', etc. (II, prologue; p. 465).

13 R. D. F. Pring-Mill, 'Some techniques of representation in the *Sueños* and the *Criticón*', *Bulletin of Hispanic Studies*, 45 (1968), 275–7, offers an excellent analysis of the context of the last phrase quoted here, in which he examines the interaction of different points of view.

14 Mateo Alemán, *Ortografía castellana*, ed. J. Rojas Garcidueñas, with a prologue by T. Navarro (Mexico, 1950), p. 109. On the symbolism of the letter *Y* in literary tradition there is a brief reference in *La novela picaresca española*, vol. I, p. 123, n. 80, [and further bibliography in my book *Vida u obra de Petrarca*, vol. I: *Lectura del 'Secretum'* (Padua/Chapel Hill, 1974), pp. 304–6].

15 See Moreno Báez, *Lección y sentido*, pp. 106–9, which contains highly relevant material and interpretations.

16 Compare Cros, *Protée et le gueux*, pp. 360–2, and Green, *Spain and the Western Tradition*, vol. IV, p. 228, n. 40.

17 Compare also the valuable analysis by A. A. Parker in *Literature and the Delinquent. The Picaresque Novel in Spain and Europe, 1599–1753* (Edinburgh, 1967), pp. 42–3. See also now the important prologue by Maurice Molho in *Romans picaresques espagnols* (Paris, 1968), pp. xliv–xlix, which unfortunately reached me too late for me to take advantage of it as it deserves. [Molho's study has been published in Spanish as a separate volume: *Introducción al pensamiento picaresco* (Salamanca, 1972).]

18 Francisco Ynduráin devotes some very well judged pages to the *Guzmán* in 'La novela desde la segunda persona. Análisis estructural', an essay included in the collection *Prosa novelesca actual* (Madrid, 1968), pp. 177–80. [Now see also Gonzalo Sobejano, 'De Alemán a Cervantes: monólogo y diálogo', in *Homenaje al prof. Muñoz Cortés* (Murcia, 1977), pp. 713–29.]

19 [I can only deplore the fact that precisely the type of nonsense whose dangers I took care to avoid should have led more than one writer to deny Guzmán's conversion. Thus Joan Arias, *Guzmán de Alfarache, The Unrepentant Narrator* (London, 1977), presents a sort of counter-novel, which has been constructed starting from certain suggestions from Mateo Alemán, and in which she expounds her personal opinions as to what should have been the behaviour of a 'repentant narrator' (educated, presumably, at UCLA). On a more serious note, Mrs Arias's thesis can be defended only by openly contradicting the text and the context of the novel with a radical disregard or incomprehension of the types of behaviour and belief current around 1600: note merely the fact that if we took away the conversion, which is so vividly portrayed, there would not even be any reason for the very existence of a set of memoirs by Guzmán (far less one with the unique stylistic and doctrinal features of these memoirs), while on the other hand, to assert that the protagonist is deceiving us means postulating that Alemán too both intended and successfully managed to deceive his contemporaries (and many later generations). On another level, Benito Brancaforte, ed., *Guzmán de Alfarache* (Madrid, 1979), and *'Guzmán de Alfarache': ¿conversión o proceso de degradación?* (Madison, 1980), likewise denies the protagonist's conversion, relying at times on serious errors of comprehension; suffice it to note that he does not understand a word as essential in our novel as *predestinado* (I, ii, 4; p. 273) and seems to be claiming that in Alemán's Castilian and in Catholic theology it could mean something other than 'predestined for salvation': as if, according to these terms of reference, it were God who condemned the *reprobate*! Even a scholar

of such perceptive and elegant thought as Carrol B. Johnson, *Inside Guzmán de Alfarache* (Berkeley/Los Angeles, 1978), when rejecting 'the genuineness of the conversion' of Guzmán, substantiating such a rejection with three examples (p. 45), falls in each case into an anachronistic or demonstrably false interpretation, as I shall show on another occasion.]

20 See Moreno Báez, *Lección y sentido*, pp. 59–63, etc. However, I cannot agree with Professor Moreno Báez and Professor Blanco Aguinaga ('Cervantes y la picaresca. Notas sobre dos tipos de realismo', *Nueva revista de filología hispánica*, 11, 1957, 313–42), when they insist that Guzmán has two particular opportunities to reform: while he is in the service of the Cardinal and during his stay at Alcalá. This is substantially true, of course, but there is a risk of misinterpreting it: one of the messages of the novel is that salvation is possible in any situation (see *Lección y sentido*, pp. 58–9); and, as I see it, the circumstances in which Guzmán does reform are precisely the most *unfavourable*, while his drama arises from the fact that he could change his life for the better at *any* moment.

21 I say something to this effect in *La novela picaresca española*, vol. i, pp. cxl–cxli and n. 50, and I intend to return to the subject in detail. I shall just add one fact here: the crucial phrase which Alemán uses in his *San Antonio de Padua* as a synthesis of the doctrine of the efficacy of works ('for do not doubt that He who made you without you, will not save you without you', fol. 218), in the context of the obsessive problem of predestination (see Moreno Báez, *Lección y sentido*, pp. 72–5 etc.), is taken verbatim from St Augustine (compare, for example, *Castigos y documentos*, in *Biblioteca de autores españoles*, vol. li, p. 124a, and Fray M. de Córdoba, *Libro del regimiento de los señores*, in the same series, vol. clxxi, p. 160a).

22 Fray P. Malón de Chaide, *Libro de la conversión de la Magdalena*, ed. Justo García Morales (Madrid, n.d.), pp. 253–4 (see also pp. 293–4 for further points of interest for understanding the *Guzmán*).

23 *Ibid.*, p. 293.

24 Parker, in *Literature and the Delinquent*, p. 36, observes that 'as early as the second chapter Guzmán is made to point out how inappropriate are moral sentiments in his mouth, without being able to disclose that it is a repentant and not a hardened sinner who is talking'. Note, however, that once the story is properly underway and he has put his initial hesitation behind him, Guzmán makes his repentant state quite clear: 'for God has deigned to let me live long enough to mend my ways, and to give me time to reform' (ii, i, 1; p. 488); 'Like those who escape from some grave danger …, I often remember, and I never forget my evil way of life – especially that of the period just past – my lowly estate, little honour, lack of respect for God, all that time I followed such an evil path' (ii, iii, 6; p. 845), and so on. On the other hand, the reader gets to know Guzmán not only 'as the delinquent he is describing' (Parker, p. 36), but as the thoughtful, pious boy who is constantly comparing his acts with the permanent values of belief and morality. In fact, I think Guzmán apologizes for his sermons not because they come from a 'hardened sinner', but because they come from a galley slave, one of the dregs of society, suffering a punishment which not only cannot qualify him as a model worthy to be imitated, but quite the opposite: hence his continual reminders of the miseries of life in

the galleys when he is defending himself against readers' possible objections.

25 'Cervantes y la picaresca', pp. 316–28; many of the remarks made in this article could well have been included here.

26 See Moreno Báez, *Lección y sentido*, especially pp. 70–4.

27 Several of these, which are not mentioned here, are perceptively analysed by Celina Sabor de Cortazar, 'Notas para el estudio de la estructura del *Guzmán de Alfarache*' *Filología*, 8 (1962), 79–95. [Compare, in addition, Gonzalo Sobejano, 'La digresión en la prosa narrativa de Lope de Vega y en su poesía epistolar', in *Estudios ofrecidos a E. Alarcos Llorach*, vol. II (Oviedo, 1978), pp. 469–94.]

28 'I too have followed my thoughts... But since my aim is to create a perfect man, whenever I find stones suitable for the building, I collect them and pile them up' (II, i, 7; p. 557); here, of course, as in the prologue to the second part (p. 467), the 'perfect man' is none other than the mature Guzmán.

29 I devote most of my article 'Estructuras y reflejos de estructuras en el *Guzmán de Alfarache*' to illustrating and explaining the meaning and origin of this second type of discourse.

30 Compare 'Towards the poetics of the *Lazarillo*', pp. 10–15 above.

31 María Rosa Lida de Malkiel, 'Nuevas notas para la interpretación del *Libro de buen amor*', in her *Estudios de literatura española y comparada* (Buenos Aires, 1966), p. 28, n. 20, which includes other information on the didactic use of first-person form. See also my article 'Sobre el origen de la autobiografía en el *Libro de buen amor*', *Anuario de estudios medievales*, 4 (1967), 301–25, [and *Vida u obra de Petrarca*, vol. I, pp. 526–7, which contains other references].

32 As Fernando Lázaro Carreter now writes in 'Para una revisión del concepto "novela picaresca"', a paper read at the Third International Congress of Hispanists, in the plenary session on 30 August 1968, [and now published in his book *'Lazarillo de Tormes' en la picaresca*, pp. 193–229].

33 See Germán Bleiberg, 'Mateo Alemán y los galeotes', *Revista de Occidente*, 4, no. 39 (1966), 330–63; 'Nuevos datos biográficos de Mateo Alemán', in *Actas del segundo congreso internacional de hispanistas* (Nijmegen, 1967), pp. 25–49; [and 'El "informe secreto" de Mateo Alemán sobre el trabajo forzoso en las minas de Almadén', *Estudios de historia social*, 12 (1980), 357–443. Compare, on the other hand, Carrol B. Johnson, 'Mateo Alemán y sus fuentes literarias', *Nueva revista de filología hispánica*, 38 (1979), 360–74].

34 A few examples can be found in *La novela picaresca española*, vol. I, p. cxi, n. 10, [together with indications on the odd possible incongruity which does not damage the overall structure of the *Guzmán*; compare n. 8 above].

35 Salvador Clotas, 'Meditación precipitada y no premeditada sobre la novela en lengua castellana', *Cuadernos para el diálogo*, 14, special number (May, 1969), 16a.

36 I am not forgetting the caution which Francisco Ynduráin recommends in 'La novela desde la segunda persona', in the use of the term *interior monologue* in connection with the *Guzmán*.

37 See the valuable pp. 391–403 of Cros, *Protée et le gueux*; [and compare C. George Peale, '*Guzmán de Alfarache* como discurso oral', *Journal of Hispanic Philology*, 4 (1979), 25–57].

38 Both these elements occur frequently within the rich 'Christian Socratic' tradition, on which see R. Ricard, *Estudios de literatura religiosa española*

(Madrid, 1964), pp. 22–147, [and P. Courcelle's *magnum opus*, *'Connais-toi toi-même' de Socrate à Saint Bernard* (Paris, 1974–5)].

39 This has recently been well shown in connection with a characteristic theme by S. Wenzel, *The Sin of Sloth: Acedia in Medieval Thought and Literature* (Chapel Hill, 1967); [and see my *Vida u obra de Petrarca*, vol. i, pp. 128 ff.].

40 Compare, for example, the final chapter of J. Leclerq, *L'amour des lettres et le désir de Dieu. Initiation aux auteurs monastiques du Moyen Age* (Paris, 1957), [or Rafael Lapesa, 'Un ejemplo de prosa retórica a fines del siglo xiv: los *Soliloquios* de fray Pedro Fernández Pecha', in his book *Poetas y prosistas de ayer y de hoy* (Madrid, 1977), pp. 9–24].

41 See Lida de Malkiel, *La originalidad artística de 'La Celestina'*, pp. 727–8.

42 Compare n. 20 above.

43 I do not think Professor Parker is right when he takes Carlos Blanco Aguinaga to task for considering 'original sin to be some force that "determines" human free-will to further sin' (*Literature and the Delinquent*, p. 154); precisely what is meant by 'determines' should perhaps be clarified, but it does seem true to say that Alemán carries the consequences of original sin to such extremes that he almost threatens to undermine the doctrine of free will, at the very limits of Catholic orthodoxy: see T. Hanrahan, SJ, *La mujer en la novela picaresca de Mateo Alemán* (Madrid, 1964), pp. 66–8; *La novela picaresca española*, i, pp. cxxxvii and cxli, n. 49.

44 One very typical example will serve to illustrate this: 'I said to myself as I thought it over: "If I feel this little trick so acutely, merely because it was a trick, how must it have been for my relatives when I played that really nasty one on them?"' (ii, iii, 2; p. 753).

45 On the title of the work, in which *atalaya* should be understood as 'a lookout or sentry who observes from a watchtower', see *La novela picaresca española*, vol. i, pp. cv–cvi, cxlvii, clxxix, n. 2.

46 Blanco Aguinaga, 'Cervantes y la picaresca', pp. 313–42, and some of my own observations in 'Estructuras y reflejos de estructuras en el *Guzmán de Alfarache*', pp. 182–4 (a study in which I offer a reading of the novel which complements these pages: there I start from the 'opinions', the least 'novelistic' element; here I concentrate predominantly on the 'life', the narrative keys).

3 The picaresque novel and the point of view

1 A diametrically opposite view is defended by my esteemed friend A. Rumeau, to whom we owe a masterly study of the early texts of the novel: 'Notes au *Lazarillo*', *Bulletin hispanique*, 66 (1964), 257–93. Rumeau is supported by Claudio Guillén, 'Luis Sánchez, Ginés de Pasamonte y los inventores del género picaresco', in *Homenaje a Rodríguez-Moñino* (Madrid, 1966), vol. i, pp. 221–3 (an article which in other respects I find extremely well judged). Here I offer only a sample of the reasons which lead me to adopt a different position on this problem.

2 In addition to the work by A. Rumeau cited in the previous note, see the introduction to the critical edition by J. Caso González (Madrid, 1967), pp. 14–22. [Maxime Chevalier, *Lectura y lectores en la España del siglo XVI y XVII* (Madrid, 1976), pp. 167–97, documents the existence of a lost edition

(Valencia, 1589), and includes some valuable reflections on the subject under discussion in the present section.]

3 Compare *La novela picaresca española*, vol. I, pp. xvii–xviii, [as well as my 1980 edition of the *Lazarillo*, p. 87, n. 12; and Noël Salomon, 'Algunos problemas de sociología de las literaturas de lengua española', in *Creación y público en la literatura española*, ed. J.-F. Botrel and S. Salaün (Madrid, 1974), pp. 27–8].

4 See Rumeau, 'Notes au *Lazarillo*', p. 274.

5 See my 'Problemas del *Lazarillo*', p. 289, n. 30 for details.

6 A text cited by A. Rumeau, *Le 'Lazarillo de Tormes'. Essai d'interprétation, essai d'attribution* (Paris, 1964), p. 32.

7 Margherita Morreale, *Pedro Simón Abril* (Madrid, 1949), p. 157.

8 In *Diálogos familiares de la agricultura cristiana* (Salamanca, 1589); the references to the *Lazarillo* are listed in the useful introduction by P. J. Meseguer Fernández to the edition in the *Biblioteca de autores españoles*, vol. CXLI (Madrid, 1963), p. cvii, n. 105.

9 See *La novela picaresca española*, vol. I, [and my 1980 *Lazarillo*], pp. xxviii–xxix.

10 L. de Góngora, *Sonetos completos*, ed. Biruté Ciplijauskaité (Madrid, Clásicos Castalia, 1969), p. 161. Line 9 should perhaps be emended to read 'que me guía' ('who guides me'); if not, *enviar* ('send') should be construed in the strictly etymological sense of 'lead along the road'. In fact I think the same elaborate word-play is involved here as in the *Lazarillo*, p. 67: 'being blind, he enlightened me and guided me [that is, led me by the hand, conducting me] along the highway of life' ('siendo ciego, me alumbró y adestró en la carrera de vivir'): a word-play (obviously derived from Matthew 15. 14, etc.) which constitutes one of the novel's most important points of reference, [recognized as such by Luis Barahona de Soto (d. 1595) in his *Diálogos de la montería*], though it came outside the scope of my argument in chapter 1.

11 Recently Professor José Caso González has ventured an interesting hypothesis, according to which the *Lazarillo* of 1554 was an extract from an early *Libro de Lázaro de Tormes*, which supposedly consisted entirely of a lucianic novel of transformations; see his article 'La génesis del *Lazarillo de Tormes*', *Archivum*, 16 (1966), 129–55 [Antonio Llull, *De oratione libri septem*, Basle, n.d. (but dedicated to Philip II), p. 502, was probably thinking of the Antwerp, 1555, continuation when he wrote that the 'dialogus' is akin 'ad poemam quod vocant "dramaticum", licet una aliquando tantum persona loquatur, ut docent Apuleius, Lucianus, Lazarillus'; compare García Berrio, *Formación de la teoría literaria moderna*, II, p. 51.]

12 See K. P. Chapman, '*Lazarillo de Tormes*, a jest-book and Benedik', *Modern Language Review*, 55 (1960), 565–7.

13 Compare Lida de Malkiel, 'Función del cuento popular en el *Lazarillo de Tormes*', p. 365, n. 12.

14 J. de Timoneda, *Obras*, vol. II (Madrid, 1948), p. 331.

15 See, respectively, Fray I. de Buendía, *Triunfo de llaneza*, ed. E. M. Wilson (Madrid, 1970), p. 69; Robert Jammes, *Études sur l'oeuvre poétique de ... Góngora ...* (Bordeaux, 1967), pp. 71–2; *Colección de autos, farsas y coloquios del siglo XVI* (Barcelona/Madrid, 1901), p. 363; '*Entreacto*', *Boletín de la Real Academia Española*, 15 (1928), 175–7; E. de Salazar, *Cartas*, ed. F. R. C. Maldonado (Madrid, 1966), p. 124. [For other reminiscences of the *Lazarillo* before the publication of the *Guzmán*, see Eugenio Asensio, 'Dos obras

dialogadas con influencias del *Lazarillo de Tormes*: *Coloquios*, de Collazos, y anónimo, *Diálogo del Capón*', *Cuadernos hispanoamericanos*, nos. 280–2 (Oct.–Dec. 1973), and 'Damasio de Frías y su *Dórida*, diálogo de amor. El italianismo en Valladolid', *Nueva revista de filología hispánica*, 24 (1975), 219–34; Chevalier, *Lectura y lectores*; and, for example, my 1980 *Lazarillo*, p.114.]

16 A phrase coined by Marcel Bataillon in *Le roman picaresque* (Paris, 1931), p. 15.

17 A monograph is needed on the early history of this term, apparently coined in the eighteenth century; [for the present, one can consult M. Nerlich, 'Plädoyer für Lázaro: Bemerkungen zu einer Gattung', *Romanische Forschungen*, 80 (1968), 354–94].

18 See chapter 2, n. 45 above.

19 Umberto Eco, *Apocalittici e integrati*, third edition (Milan, 1974), p. 203. [It is perhaps worth recalling the Aristotelian background to the quotation: 'Unity in a fable does not mean, as some think, that it has one man for its subject. To any one man many things happen – an infinite number – and some of them do not make any sort of unity; and in the same way one man has many doings which cannot be made into a unit of action' (*Poetics*, VIII, translated by L. J. Potts, *Aristotle on the Art of Fiction*, Cambridge, 1968, p. 28).]

20 The most important investigation on the origin of the word [is now Yakov Malkiel, 'El núcleo del problema etimológico de *pícaro-picardía*. En torno al proceso de préstamo doble', in *Studia hispanica in honorem R. Lapesa*, vol. II (Madrid, 1974), pp. 307–42].

21 Cited by Agustín González de Amezúa, *Cervantes, creador de la novela corta española*, vol. II (Madrid, 1958), p. 73.

22 Cristóbal Pérez de Herrera, *Discursos del amparo de los legítimos pobres* (Madrid, 1598), fol. 52v, mentions 'the source of so many *pícaros* and wanton girls that these [female vagrants] provide for commonwealths, by abandoning them at the doors of churches and houses, or bringing up those that stay with them in so depraved and undisciplined a way that they are difficult to control and convert to good behaviour afterwards'. [See now the valuable edition prepared by Michel Cavillac (Madrid, 1975), pp. 128–9.]

23 See Amezúa, *Cervantes*, pp. 76–9, although it is by no means necessarily true that 'the *pícaro* was born in … seigneurial kitchens'. [Compare Malkiel, 'El núcleo del problema etimológico de *pícaro-picardía*', pp. 339–42, and Charles V. Aubrun, 'Los avatares del pícaro de cocina', in *Sprache und Geschichte. Festschrift für Harry Meier* (Munich, 1971), pp. 17–29.]

24 In this connection, the study by F. de Haan, 'Pícaros y ganapanes', in *Homenaje a Menéndez Pelayo* (Madrid, 1899), vol. II, pp. 149–90, is still of fundamental importance.

25 Cited by Miguel Herrero García, *Madrid en el teatro* (Madrid, 1963), p. 22.

26 'La vida del ganapán', a little anonymous poem published by R. Foulché-Delbosc, *Revue hispanique*, 9 (1902), 291–2; the date is clear from a reference to the Cortes of Monzón.

27 S. de Covarrubias, *Tesoro de la lengua castellana*, ed. Martín de Riquer (Barcelona, 1943), p. 869a. [Compare José Antonio Maravall, 'Relaciones de dependencia e integración social: criados, graciosos y pícaros', *Ideologies and Literature*, 1, no. 4 (1977), 3–32; and chapter 1, n. 57 above.]

28 Maldonado, ed., Salazar, *Cartas*, p. 16. Compare J. Scudieri Ruggieri, '*Picacantones* e *pícaros de corte*: contributo alla storia del mondo picaresco', in *Studi di letteratura spagnola* (Rome, 1965), pp. 211–23.

29 M. de Cervantes, *Novelas ejemplares*, ed. R. Schevill and A. Bonilla, vol. II (Madrid, 1923), pp. 268–9.

30 Compare Luis Maristany, 'La concepción barojiana de la figura del golfo', *Bulletin of Hispanic Studies*, 45 (1968), 102–22.

31 See the essential studies by Bataillon: 'Les nouveaux chrétiens dans l'essor du roman picaresque', 'L'honneur et la matière picaresque', and '"La picaresca". À propos de *La pícara Justina*', [and José Antonio Maravall, *Poder, honor y élites en el siglo XVII* (Madrid, 1979), pp. 11–145].

32 See the corresponding texts in *La novela picaresca española*, vol. I, pp. cxii–cxxvii.

33 It is just when Alemán is presenting his character engaged in the activity which at that time epitomized the essence of the picaresque, as an errand boy, that he portrays him as someone very different from ordinary messengers: thoughtful, pious, honest. The contrast points to one of the main theses of the work ('you can achieve salvation in your own estate', I, ii, 4; p. 275, however wretched it may be), underlines human freedom and individualizes Guzmán (the individual takes precedence over the type, not the other way round). Alemán cannot have been pleased that the title *Pícaro* became widely used to refer to the protagonist (and the novel): on the contrary, he attempted to make Guzmán a complex character, a sort of battlefield of picaresque and non-picaresque traits (the 'little honour' of the *pícaro* and the desire for honour, the *pícaro*'s roguery and his virtuous inclinations, and so on).

34 See also the important letter discovered and published by Cros, *Protée et le gueux*, p. 438, [even though its attribution to Alemán and its true date are debatable points].

35 'The title *pícaro* ... is also extended to cover his life as a servant, a student, a false gentleman, a swindler and a scoundrel; because at none of these times does he stop being the rogue, that is, the *pícaro* that is announced right from the preliminaries of the book', as Lázaro Carreter writes in his fundamental study 'Para una revisión del concepto "novela picaresca"'.

36 See Mariano Baquero Goyanes, 'El entremés y la novela picaresca', in *Estudios dedicados a Menéndez Pidal*, vol. VI (Madrid, 1956), pp. 215–46; Frida Weber de Kurlat, *Lo cómico en el teatro de Fernán González de Eslava* (Buenos Aires, 1963), pp. 149–80; [or, for a study of greater critical penetration, Aurora Egido, 'Retablo carnavalesco del buscón don Pablos', *Hispanic Review*, 46 (1978), 173–97].

37 Quoted from Asensio, *Itinerario del entremés*, p. 31: here and elsewhere in his book one will find a very fine critical analysis of many types of subject matter common to the theatre and the novel.

38 Take, for example, the *Entremés de los gatillos* by Moreto (in *Verdores del Parnaso*, Madrid, 1668, pp. 167–84). This little work shows us two 'ragged little *pícaros*' on stage; but the plot in which they figure presents them to us rather as *gatillos*, or young thieves, accomplished tricksters, embodiments of a literary and real-life archetype much older than the picaresque.

39 M. de Cervantes, *Comedias y entremeses*, ed. R. Schevill and A. Bonilla, vol. III (Madrid, 1918), pp. 139–44. The same could be said of Caramanchel in *Don*

Gil de las calzas verdes (Tirso de Molina, *Obras*, ed. Blanca de los Ríos, vol. I,
Madrid, 1946, pp. 1,606–8): here we have an adaptation of chapter 3 of the
Lazarillo (which is explicitly cited), and there are clear reminiscences of the
Guzmán (compare, for instance, p. 1,608a, and *La novela picaresca española*,
vol. I, p. 278, n. 25 and p. 843). Many parallels in seventeenth-century
drama could be cited, from Lope and Calderón to Antonio de Zamora.

40 Compare *La novela picaresca española*, vol. I, p. lxxi, n. 10 [and my 1980
   Lazarillo, p. 104, n. 54]; to the bibliography cited there the following
   should be added in particular: Parker, *Literature and the Delinquent*, pp. 6, 20,
   24 and 144, n. 13, and Lázaro Carreter, 'Para una revisión del concepto
   "novela picaresca"'; the former excludes *Lazarillo* from the canon of the
   picaresque novel, the latter argues convincingly for its inclusion. [See also
   the introduction to the Spanish edition of Parker's book *Los pícaros en la
   literatura* (Madrid, 1971), and Lázaro's reply in *Hispanic Review*, 41 (1973),
   469–97.]

41 See Bataillon, 'Les nouveaux chrétiens dans l'essor du roman picaresque',
   pp. 283–4, and 'L'honneur et la matière picaresque', pp. 486–7.

42 See Samuel Gili Gaya, *Tesoro lexicográfico*, vol. I (Madrid, 1960), p. 323.

43 Gonzalo Sobejano gives a good account of most of the ways Alemán is
   indebted to the *Lazarillo* in 'De la intención y valor del *Guzmán de Alfarache*',
   Romanische Forschungen, 71 (1959), 266–86 (reprinted in his *Forma literaria y
   sensibilidad social*, Madrid, 1967, pp. 9–34). See also McGrady, *Mateo Alemán*,
   pp. 60–6.

44 See Bataillon, '"La picaresca". À propos de *La pícara Justina*', p. 235; Lázaro
   Carreter, 'Para una revisión del concepto "novela picaresca"'; [and Maravall, 'Relaciones de dependencia e integración social'].

45 Bataillon studies several relevant aspects of this in 'Les nouveaux chrétiens
   dans l'essor du roman picaresque', pp. 286–7 (*Lazarillo*), etc.; see above,
   chapter 1, 'Towards the poetics of the *Lazarillo*'.

46 Claudio Guillén may have something similar in mind when he writes that
   'the *pícaro* is not an independent hero who can be studied *in vacuo*. If the
   picaresque story could be described through him, it would not be what we
   today call a novel. It stems, rather, from a situation or chain of situations',
   'Toward a definition of the picaresque', in *Actes du IIIe Congrès de l'Association
   Internationale de Littérature Comparée* (The Hague, 1962), p. 257, [and in his
   book *Literature as System* (Princeton, 1971), p. 77].

47 Joaquín Casalduero has rightly highlighted this point in 'Notas sobre *La
   ilustre fregona*', *Anales cervantinos*, 3 (1953), 336–7, and the article 'Cervantes',
   in *The New Catholic Encyclopedia* (there is a separate offprint); compare
   Américo Castro, *Cervantes y los casticismos españoles* (Madrid, 1966), p. 66.

48 *Novelas ejemplares*, ed. Schevill and Bonilla, p. 268. The traces of the *Guzmán*
   in *Rinconete y Cortadillo* are really important, but because they are not explicitly
   acknowledged they have generally been ignored; see the interesting article
   by José Luis Varela, 'Sobre el realismo cervantino en *Rinconete*', *Atlántida*, 6,
   no. 35 (1968), especially pp. 436–43, [reprinted in his book *La transfiguración
   literaria* (Madrid, 1970), pp. 58–70].

49 *Don Quijote*, vol. I, p. 22; ed. Martín de Riquer (Barcelona, 1962), p. 227.

50 Compare chapter 1, n. 3 above.

51 Information on most of these subjects will be found in *La novela picaresca*

española, vol. I; and in Moreno Báez, *Lección y sentido*; McGrady, *Mateo Alemán*; Cros, *Protée et le gueux*.

52 See Claudio Guillén's intelligent comments in 'Luis Sánchez, Ginés de Pasamonte y los inventores del género picaresco'.

53 I quote from the edition by J. Puyol y Alonso (Madrid, 1912; numbers in the text refer to volume and page). [The more recent one by A. Rey Hazas (Madrid, 1977) is useful.]

54 See Bataillon, '"La picaresca". À propos de *La pícara Justina*', pp. 240–50. Justina declares herself to be a '*pícara* through and through, not like others who ... at the least sign of trouble become messengers, people who, unable to find a master, lo and behold, turn into *pícaros*: and, once they're in that profession, live uncomfortably and go around sad, against all principles of roguery. I shall demonstrate how I have been a *pícara* from birth ..., a confirmed, inveterate *pícara*.' Even at the risk of harping on a theme already dealt with previously, it is worth highlighting this passage, which is very representative of the paradoxical confusion in which the picaresque novel arose. Justina, no doubt thinking of Guzmán, denies the errand boy the title of *pícaro*, contrary to common usage at the end of the sixteenth century and contrary to Alfarache himself; on the other hand, she always calls the protagonist of the *Watchtower* 'Pícaro' when she refers to him in general terms. Alemán reserved the name for one transitory situation Guzmanillo passes through: López de Úbeda applies it to a lifelong, even hereditary disposition. This displacement shapes the novelistic *pícaro* as a literary creation.

55 Several of these have already been cited. [The whole series has been published in one volume, in Spanish, as *Pícaros y picaresca*.]

56 *Pícaros y picaresca*, pp. 45–6. I have abridged this passage merely in order to avoid complementary explanations, not because I disagree with the statements omitted here.

57 One which it has in *Marcos de Obregón* (which is obviously not a picaresque novel, either as regards character or structure, even though it owes quite a lot to the genre); see G. Haley, *Vicente Espinel and Marcos de Obregón. A Life and Its Literary Representation* (Providence, Rhode Island, 1959), pp. 65–82.

58 I have used the splendid critical edition by Fernando Lázaro Carreter (Salamanca, 1965). [Those by B. W. Ife (Oxford, 1977) and Domingo Ynduráin (Madrid, 1980) are also valuable, for their introductions and notes.]

59 See the critical edition already cited, pp. lii–lv. It could be argued that the work was perhaps not completed until 1605: Quevedo seems, in fact, to have had in mind certain features of the second part of the *Guzmán*, which appeared in December of the previous year; [but there is sufficient evidence to indicate that this second part had previously circulated in manuscript, at least in the version known to 'Mateo Luján de Sayavedra', the author of the apocryphal continuation. See also below, postscript, n. 11]. On the other hand, the text was revised, probably between 1609 and 1614, as Professor Lázaro Carreter conjectures.

60 Lázaro Carreter, 'Para una revisión del concepto "novela picaresca"' [and 'Quevedo: la invención por la palabra', in *Academia Literaria Renacentista*, vol. II: *Homenaje a Quevedo* (Salamanca, 1982), pp. 8–24. The essays of Raimundo Lida, now revised and brought together in his book *Prosas de Quevedo*

(Barcelona, 1980), are fundamental in this connection; on the *Buscón*, see especially pp. 239–304].

61 See Leo Spitzer, 'Zur Kunst Quevedos in seinem *Buscón*', in *Romanische Stil- und Literaturstudien*, vol. II (Marburg, 1931), especially pp. 74–8 [a study now available in Spanish in G. Sobejano, ed., *Francisco de Quevedo* (Madrid, 1978), pp. 123–84], and *Lingüística e historia literaria* (Madrid, 1955), pp. 325–6. Compare Asensio, *Itinerario del entremés*, pp. 178–96, which contains some very shrewd observations on the subject. Professor Asensio, p. 190, makes a penetrating comparison between Quevedo and Arcimboldo. It is worth recalling that Arcimboldo was attracting attention in Spain during the period when Quevedo was writing his novel. Thus Fray Pedro de Valder- rama writes in his *Ejercicios espirituales para todos los días de la Cuaresma (Primera, segunda y tercera parte)* (Zaragoza, 1605), fol. 56: 'You have seen some paintings done with such artifice, now for the first time, that seen from a distance, they have a face with a craggy nose, blurred eyes, an unkempt beard, a turban on the head, that truly instils fear and horror. But look closely: it is all made of fruit and flowers, the nose is a cucumber, the eyes are figs, the moustaches are broad beans, the ears are mushrooms and the head is a basket; the whole thing is edible, the whole thing is a hamper of fruit, and some others are flowers.' [Compare Edmond Cros, *Ideología y genética textual. El caso del 'Buscón'* (Madrid, 1980), p. 44, etc.]

62 Here I regretfully disagree with Harry Sieber, 'Apostrophes in the *Buscón*: an approach to Quevedo's narrative technique', *Modern Language Notes*, 83 (1968), 181–4, an otherwise excellent article. I think Professor Sieber points out the facts well, but to evaluate them properly requires a comparison between how they function in Quevedo and in his models: in the *Buscón*, their loss of meaning is absolute.

63 See the fundamental study by Fernando Lázaro Carreter, 'Originalidad del *Buscón*', in *Studia philologica. Homenaje a Dámaso Alonso*, vol. II (Madrid, 1960), pp. 319–38 [and also the well-judged pages lxxxv–lxxxvi of the study by Molho, prologue to *Romans picaresques espagnols*, as well as his more disputable 'Cinco lecciones sobre el *Buscón*', in his book *Semántica y poética (Góngora, Quevedo)* (Barcelona, 1977), pp. 89–131].

64 'Quevedo has not created him merely to group around a wide range of people against the changing backcloth of society', writes C. B. Morris, *The Unity and Structure of Quevedo's Buscón: 'Desgracias encadenadas'* (Hull, 1965), p. 6. My interpretation is almost diametrically opposed to this; I say *almost*, because I believe that Quevedo's ultimate goal is not Pablos, nor 'a wide range of people', but the use of both as a fuse for the fireworks of his wit. In any case, it seems certain to me that the possible unity of the *Buscón* is not derived from the coherence of Pablos as a character. [Among the most recent contrib- utions, I agree in general with the evaluations of the work advanced by Lida in *Prosas de Quevedo*; Ife and Ynduráin in their critical editions; Michel and Cecile Cavillac in 'A propos du *Buscón* et du *Guzmán de Alfarache*', *Bulletin his- panique*, 75 (1973), 114–31; E. Williamson in 'The conflict between author and protagonist in Quevedo's *Buscón*', *Journal of Hispanic Philology*, 2 (1977), 45–59; for further observations see postscript below.]

65 Naturally, if one's starting point is that 'novels ... should tell us something important about human nature and human life', and one wishes (quite

properly) to defend the exceptional artistic quality of the *Buscón* without denying it its status as a novel, but also without revising that narrow-minded idea of the *genre*, there is no alternative but to turn Quevedo's work, against all the evidence, into the product of 'a serious interest in delinquency', into 'a profoundly moral story ... a novel rich in human truth, one that gives us a psychological study of a delinquent that is far in advance of its time', and so on. So it is with Parker, *Literature and the Delinquent*, pp. 9, 58 and 62, and various British critics following him (see Parker, pp. 162–3).

66 Here I do agree with Morris, *The Unity and Structure of Quevedo's 'Buscón'*, and Parker, *Literature and the Delinquent*, p. 61. But I say *a part*, not *the whole*: Pablos throws himself more than once, without the slightest reflection or consistency, into situations that are irreconcilable with his ambition. It is obvious that this most typical feature of his personality is conceived from the outside, in order to point out the grotesque nature of the figure, and not recreated from within, taken seriously. Quevedo does not aim to probe 'the inner, deep-seated motives that make a delinquent choose that manner of life rather than another' (Parker, p. 62); such motives, for him, boil down to just one: heredity (compare Castro, *Hacia Cervantes*, pp. 117–18); and he takes pleasure in demonstrating this, comically, by making Pablos come to grief time and again in the face of his hereditary destiny. [Compare also Molho, prologue to *Romans picaresques espagnols*, pp. xcvi–civ; Cavillac, 'À propos du *Buscón* et du *Guzmán de Alfarache*'; Williamson, 'The conflict between author and protagonist in Quevedo's *Buscón*', with all of whom I am happy to find myself essentially in agreement.]

67 We already know the importance of the references in the *Lazarillo* and the *Guzmán* to the time at which the protagonists are writing; in the *Buscón* there is nothing of this sort: this is shown beyond doubt by the references collected by Sieber, 'Apostrophes in the *Buscón*', pp. 209–10.

68 I hope it will not seem too ingenuous of me to state this explicitly; according to Professor Parker, *Literature and the Delinquent*, p. 66, the episode is decisive for the 'psychological study' of the character: it reveals 'his self-identification with his mother's guilt'; quite frankly, all I can see here is that Pablos is conceived in a grotesque mode, without the slightest desire for psychological realism. Compare Bataillon, *Défense et illustration du sens littéral*, pp. 27–30. [Now one can also consult the introduction to the Spanish edition of Parker's book, and the reply from Lázaro Carreter, 'Glosas críticas a *Los pícaros en la literatura*', as well as Antonio Gargano's introduction to his edition of the novel (Barcelona, 1982).]

69 Lázaro Carreter, 'Originalidad del *Buscón*', p. 335. Compare Ian Watt's remarks on *Moll Flanders* in *The Rise of the Novel* (Berkeley, 1962), p. 98.

70 As he does especially on pp. 238–41; compare *La novela picaresca española*, vol. I, p. lxvi.

71 [1604 (without further details) is the date which appears on the dedication of *El Guitón Honofre*, the work of a certain *licenciado* Gregorio González. In 1967, thanks to my dear friend Juan Bautista Avalle-Arce, I obtained temporary access to the manuscript of this work, which is preserved in the library of Smith College, Northampton, Mass.; my knowledge of the novel, however, was then too slight for me to do more than briefly mention it in a note in the Spanish edition of the present book. Since then, the *Guitón* has been edited

(albeit unsatisfactorily) by H. Genéreux Carrasco (Valencia, Estudios de Hispanófila, 1973). I am now, therefore, in a position to indicate that unfortunately González's book serves precisely to confirm my observations on the 'dead-end street' that the picaresque entered after the *Guzmán*. The protagonist himself openly (and rather incongruously) declares his affiliations: 'since there is a first *pícaro* and a second, it is right to give them a companion, for the world cannot manage without a vagabond [*guitón*]' (p. 112). There is no way of deciding whether he is alluding to Lázaro and Guzmán, to Mateo Alemán's Guzmán and that of 'Luján de Sayavedra', or even to the first (1599) and second (1604) parts of Alemán's work (he could have known this last in manuscript, as he doubtless knew the *Buscón*: see n. 59 above and postscript, n. 11; for the genealogy of the *guitón*, see my *Primera cuarentena*, Barcelona, 1982, § XIX). But the phrase strikes me as a clear symptom of what the work actually is: a third-rate derivative of the genre in fashion. Page after page, the *Guitón* is a hotchpotch of elements, extremely crudely cobbled together, from the *Lazarillo* and the two versions of *Guzmán*. Alemán, especially, is raided by González with blind persistence: one moment it occurs to him to imitate *sententiae* from the *Guzmán*, then a situation, then proverbs or a feature of the characters; but always carelessly, without any plan, improvising at random (and, at best, correcting himself as he goes along: one need only read what is said in chapter 8 on the subject of Honofre's possible conversion). This constant process of depredation does not exclude some of the factors in which the refined technique of point of view in the *Guzmán* was most obviously crystallized; these factors, however, accord neither with each other nor with the other ingredients plagiarized indiscriminately from one source or another. There is no point in giving examples: the mere fact that the novel remained unpublished suggests in itself that what we have here is perhaps the nadir of the Spanish picaresque. Nevertheless, it does show us, in the raw state, a fair number of what seemed in the period to be the conventional constituent elements of the picaresque genre, and thus, in its very wretchedness, and precisely because of the absolute lack of any ability to link these elements together, it is of some interest.]

72 See above, pp. 68–9 and notes 50 to 51.

73 Compare del Monte, *Itinerario del romanzo picaresco spagnolo*, pp. 80–2.

74 See A. Carballo Picazo, 'El doctor Carlos García, novelista español del siglo XVII', *Revista bibliográfica y documental*, 5 (1951), 5–46, [and Ricardo Senabre, 'El doctor Carlos García y la picaresca', *Cuadernos para la investigación de la literatura hispánica*, 1 (1978), 43–54].

75 See pp. 64–5 and 67–8 above. [If in *Pedro de Urdemalas* we are dealing with a *pícaro* without a novel, in the *Coloquio de los perros*, for example, we find ourselves with picaresque novel forms, but without a *pícaro*. Compare, however, Gonzalo Sobejano, 'El *Coloquio de los perros* en la picaresca y otros apuntes', *Hispanic Review*, 43 (1975), 25–41.]

76 See, for example, Cros, *Protée et le gueux*, pp. 412–16, and *Contribution à l'étude des sources de 'Guzmán de Alfarache'* (Montpellier, 1967), pp. 80–3; *La novela picaresca española*, vol. I, pp. 365, n. 17, and 866, n. 15.

77 Such as *El necio bien afortunado* (1621), or, even more remote from the genre of the novel, two works which are a mixture of poetry and theatre: *El sutil*

cordobés Pedro de Urdemalas (1620) and *La sabia Flora malsabidilla* (1621); all three are by this same Salas Barbadillo.

78 Most recently edited, together with the other little novels that accompany it in the original volume, by G. E. Sansone (Barcelona, 1960), [and, with a new introduction and notes, in the collection Clásicos Castellanos (Madrid, 1974)].

79 The relevant bibliography and a series of observations on this work will be found in J. L. Laurenti, *Vida de Lazarillo de Tormes. Estudio crítico de la Segunda Parte de Juan de Luna* (Mexico, 1965), [and in his edition in Clásicos Castellanos (Madrid, 1979)]. In addition, I would draw attention to the elegant edition with introduction by M. de Riquer, *La Celestina y Lazarillos* (Barcelona, 1959); see also Marcel Bataillon in *Bulletin hispanique*, 62 (1960), 340, [and R. S. Rudder, 'Nueva luz sobre Juan de Luna', in the volume *La picaresca* (Madrid, 1979), pp. 485–91].

80 See *La novela picaresca española*, vol. I, p. clxxxi and n. 7.

81 Published in vol. XVIII of the *Biblioteca de autores españoles*, which also contains the next work cited here, [now also available in the edition by Arsenio Pacheco (Madrid, 1975)].

82 For a sample of such works, see the collection selected by José María de Cossío in vol. XC of the *Biblioteca de autores españoles*.

83 [Compare Gonzalo Sobejano, 'Un perfil de la picaresca: el pícaro hablador', in *Studia hispanica in honorem R. Lapesa*, vol. II (Madrid, 1975), pp. 467–85.]

84 See P. N. Dunn's notable book *Castillo Solórzano and the Decline of the Spanish Novel* (Oxford, 1952).

85 Along with *Periquillo, el de las gallineras* (1668), by Francisco Santos, in which, moreover, the abandonment of autobiography is consistent with the conversion of the hero into a character who scarcely retains any features of the literary *pícaro* (and instead conforms entirely to the tradition of the mendicant philosopher: Apollonius, Diogenes, Aesop ...).

86 The same is true to a much worse extent of the appalling *Novela del licenciado Periquín*, included by Juan Cortés de Tolosa among his *Discursos morales* (1617), and now reprinted in the work cited in n. 78 above.

87 I. S. Révah provides much new information on this author in 'Un pamphlet contre l'Inquisition d'Antonio Enríquez Gómez: la seconde partie de la *Política angélica*', *Revue des études juives*, 131 (1962), 81–168. [See now the edition of *El siglo pitagórico y Vida de don Gregorio Guadaña* carefully prepared by Charles Amiel (Paris, 1977).]

88 See W. K. Jones in *Revue hispanique*, 77 (1929), 201–45; E. R. Moore and A. S. Bates in *Hispanic Review*, 8 (1940), 24–45 and 63–6, respectively; [and now, in particular, Marcel Bataillon, 'Estebanillo González, bouffon pour rire', in *Studies in Spanish Literature of the Golden Age presented to E. M. Wilson* (London, 1973), pp. 25–44, and Franco Meregalli, 'La existencia de Estebanillo González', *Revista de literatura*, 41 (1979), 55–67].

89 Parker, *Literature and the Delinquent*, pp. 76–7; J. Goytisolo, 'Estebanillo González, hombre de buen humor', in his book *El furgón de cola* (Paris, 1967), pp. 60–76, [and Barcelona, 1976, pp. 95–120].

90 Covarrubias, *Tesoro*, ed. Riquer, p. 981a. [See now D. Pamp de Avalle-Arce, introduction to Francesillo de Zúñiga, *Crónica burlesca del emperador Carlos V* (Barcelona, 1981), pp. 23–35, 48–56, and the *thèse* by Monique Joly, *La bourle*

et son interprétation. Recherches sur le passage de la facétie au roman (Espagne XVIe–XVIIe siècles) (Montpellier, 1979).]

91 I quote from the edition by J. Millé y Jiménez (Madrid, 1934; numbers in the text refer to volume and page), [now superseded, however, by that of A. Carreira and J. A. Cid (Madrid, 1971)].

92 Compare Rico, 'Sobre el origen de la autobiografía en el *Libro de buen amor*', pp. 324–5.

93 G. de Vinsauf, in Edmond Faral, *Les arts poétiques du XIIe et du XIIIe siècle* (Paris, 1958), p. 87. See above, p. 2 and n. 2; p. 16 and n. 33; p. 53 and n. 41.

94 John of Garland, *ibid.*

95 C. Suárez de Figueroa, *El pasajero*, ed. Francisco Rodríguez Marín (Madrid, 1913), p. 78. The whole context deserves to be quoted here; let me just reproduce one fragment: 'you must know that comedy is ... humble, as regards the action, those who make up the comic fiction being plebeian or, at most, townspeople ... It follows from this (writes a grammarian) that it is a mistake to include the actions of illustrious characters in [comic] fiction because they are unable to provoke laughter, for laughter must necessarily be produced by humble folk. The incidents, struggles and disputes of the latter delight their audience. This is not true of the quarrels of nobles. If a prince is made fun of, he at once takes offence and is aggrieved; the offence requires vengeance, vengeance causes violent upheavals and disastrous outcomes, which take one into the domain of the tragic...'. [Compare Antonio García Berrio, *Introducción a la poética clasicista: Cascales* (Barcelona, 1975), pp. 339–46, especially for quotation of and commentary on passages in which Suárez de Figueroa and Cascales coincide almost literally.]

96 Parker adopts a very different view, *Literature and the Delinquent*, pp. 25–7.

97 Compare again Lázaro Carreter, 'Originalidad del *Buscón*', pp. 335–6; Bataillon, *Défense et illustration du sens littéral*, pp. 28–9.

98 See Erich Auerbach, *Mimesis: The Representation of Reality in Western Literature* (Princeton, 1953), a work which is not always reliable, however. [See postscript, pp. 292–3 and n. 1.]

99 While the original Spanish edition of this book was in press I was able, through the kindness of Harry Sieber, to read Stuart Miller, *The Picaresque Novel* (Cleveland, 1967), which includes a chapter (pp. 97–127) on 'Point of view, style, and the ending of the picaresque novel'; Professor Miller devotes sections to the *Lazarillo, The Unfortunate Traveller, Guzmán, Buscón, Simpliciss-imus, Gil Blas, Moll Flanders* and *Roderick Random*: in general, his approach and conclusions bear virtually no relation to my own.

Postscript

1 The commentary on the context of this quotation in Auerbach, *Mimesis* is one of the best chapters (no. 19) in that work; the remarks recently devoted to it by J. Bruck, 'From Aristotelian mimesis to "bourgeois" realism', *Poetics*, 11 (1982), 189–202, will be of interest to some; but I greatly prefer the masterly pages (64–73) in which it is discussed in Harry Levin, *The Gates of Horn* (New York, 1963).

2 I am more and more convinced that he withheld his name deliberately. In the Prologue, the play on the topos of the *gloriae fructus* which one can expect

to derive from a book – and which is so funny coming from Lázaro – could be interpreted as a sign that the author had the question very much in mind and had decided not to reveal his name; and interesting ideological implications and intellectual traditions can be seen in the anonymity (see my article 'Para el prólogo del *Lazarillo*').

3 See *La novela picaresca española*, vol. I, p. 95 and n. I.

4 It strikes me as indicative that the *Lazarillo* should have begun to be attributed to this or that author only after 1605 (see my 1980 edition of the *Lazarillo*, pp. xvi ff. and additional notes); before that date the character had never been distinguished from the real author: one spoke, for example, of 'Apuleius, Lucianus, Lazarillus' (see chapter 3, n. 11).

5 V. G. Mylne, *The Eighteenth-Century French Novel. Techniques of Illusion*, second edition (Cambridge, 1981), p. 11. See also *ibid.*, pp. 20–31; W. Nelson, *Fact or Fiction. The Dilemma of the Renaissance Storyteller* (Cambridge, Mass., 1973); I. Williams, *The Idea of the Novel in Europe, 1600–1800* (New York, 1979), pp. 77–83, etc. I cite these three books, out of the extensive bibliography available, because the very fact that they are estimable in themselves makes one perceive all the more clearly how much they could have benefited from a fuller and more appropriate treatment of the Spanish picaresque, and especially *Guzmán de Alfarache*, whose exceptional quality tends to be incorrectly evaluated in studies on the origins of the modern novel, even when these stop short of such inept readings as those of B. Romberg, *Studies in the Narrative Technique of the First-Person Novel* (Stockholm, 1962), or R. Démoris, *Le roman à la première personne, du classicisme aux Lumières* (Paris, 1975), which have a stereotyped mental image of the picaresque, based on the most third-rate examples of the genre, and apply it blindly to the *Guzmán*.

6 A different perspective, I hope, from the 'long-established tendency to look back to the seventeenth century not for signs of the presence of the novel as such but for signs of the techniques and attitudes which were to be developed in the novel in later periods' (Williams, *The Idea of the Novel in Europe, 1600–1800*, p. 39). Even my discussion of the *Guzmán* is set within the framework of a couple of observations drawing attention to ways in which it differs from the conventional realist novel (pp. 30–1 and 55, n. 46); and because the latter was my *historical* point of reference, I carefully pointed out quite a number of times how questionable it can be as an *aesthetic* criterion: the caveats run from the prologue to the Spanish edition right through to the final paragraph.

7 In the most recent studies, however, I think I perceive a greater interest in historical questions and in examining how far point of view 'can reveal and embody ideology' (S. S. Lanser, *The Narrative Act. Point of View in Prose Fiction*, Princeton, NJ, 1981, p. 18); 'Il termine non ha più l'originario valore prospettico (distanza e angolo da cui vengono traguardatti i fatti), ma ha piuttosto quello di concezione del mondo' (Cesare Segre, 'Punto di vista e plurivocità nell'analisi narratologica', in *Atti del convegno internazionale 'Letterature classiche e narratologia'*, Perugia, 1981, pp. 51–65). For my own part, in this little book I would not have known how to separate the structural significance of point of view from its ideological function.

8 Recently reproduced in Parker, *Literature and the Delinquent*, and R. Bjornson, *The Picaresque Hero in European Fiction* (Madison, Wisconsin, 1977).

9 An opinion I find confirmed by Alfonso Rey's observations in 'La novela
   picaresca y el narrador fidedigno', *Hispanic Review*, 47 (1979), 55–75.

10 Of course, if someone believes and writes that I branded the *Buscón* as a
   'pésima novela' [*sic*] (a 'very bad novel'), then I have nothing to say; except,
   perhaps, that to quote in this way indicates a gross lack of perception. I would
   say the same of anyone who sees a 'rejection' of my premisses – instead of
   explicit support for them – in the comments of Raimundo Lida, 'Pablos de
   Segovia y su agudeza', p. 297, n. 50 (reprinted in *Prosas de Quevedo*, p. 256, n.
   49).

11 See above, chapter 3, n. 59. The fundamental evidence is now provided by *El
   Guitón Honofre*, whose dedication is dated 1604 and which shows definite
   traces of the *Buscón*. If some points of contact may be due to a common
   tradition (see, for example, Maxime Chevalier, 'De los cuentos tradicionales
   a la picaresca', in the collection *La picaresca*, Madrid, 1979, pp. 335–45),
   others scarcely permit of any doubt: thus the fact that Guitón says 'podrán
   desterrar hoy mis dientes' 'por vagamundo[s]' (p. 73; see *Buscón*, I, 3; p. 33),
   or serves a 'señor don Diego ... que era un santico' in Alcalá (p. 132; a
   correction in the manuscript altered the University of Alcalá to that of
   Salamanca: p. 129, n. 10). Gonzalo Díaz-Migoyo, 'Las fechas en y de *El
   Buscón* de Quevedo', *Hispanic Review*, 48 (1980), 171–93, draws attention to an
   anecdote attributed to Quevedo which, together with other facts connected
   with the same subject (though these were unknown to Díaz-Migoyo) could
   set the *terminus ad quem* at 1608; but in the light of the *Guitón* it is pointless to
   dwell on so late a possible piece of evidence.

12 In the *Buscón* in general time is as plastic as in the soldier's autobiography in
   II, 3 in particular; see the judicious comments of Domingo Ynduráin, in his
   edition of the novel, pp. 63–4.

13 These words and the previous passage in quotation marks come from P. N.
   Dunn, 'Problems of a model for the picaresque and the case of Quevedo's
   Buscón', *Bulletin of Hispanic Studies*, 59 (1982), 102 and 99; if I have understood
   correctly, Professor Dunn writes these words *hypotheses fingens*, without
   necessarily presenting them as his own view.

14 See Lázaro Carreter, 'Originalidad del *Buscón*', pp. 326–33. Díaz-Migoyo,
   'Las fechas en y de *El Buscón*', pp. 178–82, falls into several errors in
   attempting to reject this dependence, in denying, for instance, *contra* Professor
   Lázaro, that Guzmán and Pablos become actors 'for love of an actress': 'por
   amores de una farsanta, quiso profesar el arte cómico' ('for love of an actress,
   he decided to join the theatrical profession'), we read in the apocryphal
   Guzmán (III, 7); and Buscón himself joins a troupe of strolling players because
   'tenía necesidad de arrimo y me había parecido bien la moza [que] hacía las
   reinas y papeles graves en la comedia' ('I needed support and protection and
   I had liked the look of the girl' who 'played the queens and the serious roles in
   the plays', III, 9). On the other hand, he compensates somewhat for mistakes
   of this sort by reproducing an accurate judgement by Gonzalo Sobejano, on
   p. 178.

15 Since it would be tedious to go back over this question here, I shall just cite a
   passage from R. Bjornson, 'Moral blindness in Quevedo's *El Buscón*', *Romanic
   Review*, 67 (1976), 57, which may serve to exemplify my 'and so on' on p. 78
   (line 24): 'Although he mocks his parents, a hermit who cheated at cards, a

vapidly pretentious poet, and a false hidalgo, he subsequently acts in precisely the same fashion as they had acted.'

16 Gonzalo Díaz-Migoyo, *Estructura de la novela. Anatomía de 'El Buscón'* (Madrid, 1978).

17 Nor those that follow it on p. 77 and reiterate it throughout the whole work. Díaz-Migoyo concurs with me in emphasizing the contradiction between the shame of the actor and the shamelessness of the fictitious author, but he considers that it is so glaring that Quevedo himself must have intended that it should be appreciated and that the reader should resolve it in the terms proposed in *Anatomía de 'El Buscón'*, by appealing to the 'para-text implicit in the author's behaviour' (p. 170 and *un peu partout*). But the inference is not admissible, either historically or artistically. Every detail of the *Lazarillo* perpetually indicates that the words of the actor and author admit of an (ironic) reading beyond the (apparent) literal meaning: for example, Lázaro is 'no … worse' than his father, or his wife is 'as good' as the other women of Toledo (see p. 22), and so on. But the details of the *Buscón*, on the other hand, refuse to allow a secondary level of reading analogous to this: Pablos always expresses his ignominious distinguishing characteristics and the jokes which highlight his degradation quite clearly, with such care as to exclude any possible invitation to construct an 'implicit para-text'. I cannot conceive of Quevedo (or the *pícaro*-writer) adopting the approach of explaining every particular (to an excessive degree, indeed) and expecting the whole thing to be interpreted as a highly complicated tacit piece of chicanery. The confirmation of Quevedo's way of proceeding (in the *Buscón* and in so many other works), of his stylistic tricks, is also what prevents me from accepting the suggestions advanced by Agustín Redondo, 'Del personaje de don Diego Coronel a una nueva interpretación de *El Buscón*', in *Actas del Quinto Congreso Internacional de Hispanistas* (Bordeaux, 1977), pp. 699–711: if Don Diego were really being denounced as a representative of rich *conversos* (converted Jews) attempting to join the nobility, Pablos would have said so as clearly and emphatically as he says similar things of other characters.

18 See the critical edition by Lázaro Carreter and the very useful one by Ife.

19 Díaz-Migoyo's answer to this problem is precisely a short chapter (pp. 72–8) which is devoted to a gloss on the 'Dedicatory Letter' and which, for all that, never mentions the fact that it is not part of the text. Other points in his study – which otherwise contains a number of interesting observations – make one appreciate likewise the dangers of a critical approach which wishes to be outside or above historical realities.

20 The three quotations in inverted commas are from Williams, *The Idea of the Novel in Europe, 1600–1800*, pp. 33, 27 and 35, respectively. See the excellent fifth chapter of Parker, *Literature and the Delinquent*.

Select bibliography

The present bibliography was compiled by Mercedes Quílez, to whom I gladly express my gratitude. It merely gathers together the studies and editions cited in the notes to the text, apart from the odd very occasional item. An adequate *mise au point* to the bibliography on the picaresque novel and an anthology of the studies on the subject will be found in *Historia y crítica de la literatura española*, ed. Francisco Rico (Barcelona, 1980–3), vol. II, pp. 340–81 (by Pedro M. Piñero), and vol. III, pp. 448–533 (by Carlos Vaíllo).

Alonso, Amado, *Materia y forma en poesía*, second edition (Madrid, 1960)
Alonso, Dámaso, *Seis calas en la expresión literaria española* (with Carlos Bousoño), second edition (Madrid, 1956)
    Pluralità e correlazione in poesia (Bari, 1971)
Amiel, Charles, ed., Antonio Enríquez Gómez, *El siglo pitagórico y Vida de don Gregorio Guadaña* (Paris, 1977)
Andrés, M., *La teología española en el siglo XVI*, vol. II (Madrid, 1976)
Arias, Joan, *Guzmán de Alfarache, The Unrepentant Narrator* (London, 1977)
Asensio, Eugenio, 'La peculiaridad literaria de los conversos', *Anuario de estudios medievales*, 4 (1967), 327–351; reprinted in *La España imaginada de Américo Castro* (Barcelona, 1976), pp. 87–117
    Itinerario del entremés (Madrid, 1965)
    'Dos obras dialogadas con influencias del *Lazarillo de Tormes: Coloquios*, de Collazos, y anónimo, *Diálogo del Capón*', *Cuadernos hispanoamericanos*, nos. 280–2 (Oct.–Dec., 1973)
    'Damasio de Frías y su *Dórida*, diálogo de amor. El italianismo en Valladolid', *Nueva revista de filología hispánica*, 24 (1975), 219–34
Aubrun, Charles V., 'Los avatares del pícaro de cocina', in *Sprache und Geschichte. Festschrift für Harry Meier* (Munich, 1971), pp. 17–29
    [Summary of his course 1953–4 at the Sorbonne], published by the FGEL (Paris, 1960)

Auerbach, Erich, *Mimesis: The Representation of Reality in Western Literature* (Princeton, 1953)

Avalle-Arce, Juan Bautista, 'Conocimiento y vida en Cervantes', *Filología*, 5 (1959), 1–34; reprinted in his *Nuevos deslindes cervantinos* (Barcelona, 1975), pp. 15–72

Baquero Goyanes, Mariano, 'El entremés y la novela picaresca', in *Estudios dedicados a Menéndez Pidal*, vol. VI (Madrid, 1956), pp. 215–46

Baron, Hans, *The Crisis of the Early Italian Renaissance* (Princeton, 1966)

Bataillon, Marcel, *Le roman picaresque* (Paris, 1931)

ed., *La vie de Lazarillo de Tormès* (Paris, 1958)

review of M. de Riquer, ed., *La Celestina y Lazarillos, Bulletin hispanique*, 62 (1960), 339–40

'L'honneur et la matière picaresque', *Annuaire du Collège de France*, 63 (1963), 458–90; available in Spanish in his work *Pícaros y picaresca*, pp. 203–14

' "La picaresca". À propos de *La pícara Justina*', in *Wort und Text. Festschrift für Fritz Schalk* (Frankfurt am Main, 1963), pp. 233–250; reprinted in *Pícaros y picaresca*, pp. 175–99

'Les nouveaux chrétiens dans l'essor du roman picaresque', *Neophilologus*, 48 (1964), pp. 283–98; reprinted in *Pícaros y picaresca*, pp. 215–43

Erasmo y España, translated by A. Alatorre, second edition (Mexico, 1966); original French edition *Érasme et l'Espagne* (Paris, 1937)

Défense et illustration du sens littéral (Leeds, 1967)

'Estebanillo González, bouffon pour rire', in *Studies in Spanish Literature of the Golden Age presented to E. M. Wilson* (London, 1973), pp. 25–44

Erasmo y el erasmismo (Barcelona, 1977)

Pícaros y picaresca, 'La pícara Justina' (Madrid, 1969)

Bates, A. S., 'Historical characters in *Estebanillo González*', *Hispanic Review*, 8 (1940), 63–6

Bjornson, R., 'Moral blindness in Quevedo's *El Buscón*', *Romanic Review*, 67 (1976), 50–9

The Picaresque Hero in European Fiction (Madison, Wisconsin, 1977)

Blanco Aguinaga, Carlos, 'Cervantes y la picaresca. Notas sobre dos tipos de realismo', *Nueva revista de filología hispánica*, 11 (1957), 313–42

Blecua, Alberto, 'Libros de caballerías, latín macarrónico y novela picaresca: la adaptación castellana del *Baldus* (Sevilla, 1542)', *Boletín de la Real Academia de Buenas Letras de Barcelona*, 34 (1971–2) 147–239

ed., *La vida de Lazarillo de Tormes y de sus fortunas y adversidades* (Madrid, 1974)

Blecua, José M., ed., Don Juan Manuel, *Obras completas*, vol. I (Madrid, 1982)

Bleiberg, Germán, 'Mateo Alemán y los galeotes', *Revista de Occidente*, 4, no. 39 (1966), 330–63

'Nuevos datos biográficos de Mateo Alemán', in *Actas del segundo congreso internacional de hispanistas* (Nijmegen, 1967), pp. 25–49

'El "informe secreto" de Mateo Alemán sobre el trabajo forzoso en las minas de Almadén', *Estudios de historia social*, 12 (1980), 357–443

Brancaforte, Benito, ed., M. Alemán, *Guzmán de Alfarache* (Madrid, 1979)

'Guzmán de Alfarache': ¿conversión o proceso de degradación? (Madison, 1980)

Bruck, J., 'From Aristotelian mimesis to "bourgeois" realism', *Poetics*, 11 (1982), 189–202

Butor, Michel, *Essais sur le roman* (Paris, 1969)

Carballo Picazo, A., 'El doctor Carlos García, novelista español del siglo XVII', *Revista bibliográfica y documental*, 5 (1951), 5–46

Caro Baroja, Julio, *Las formas complejas de la vida religiosa. Religión, sociedad y carácter en la España de los siglos XVI y XVII* (Madrid, 1978)

Carreira, A., and J. A. Cid, eds., *Estebanillo González* (Madrid, 1971)

Casalduero, Joaquín, 'Notas sobre *La ilustre fregona*', *Anales cervantinos*, 3 (1953)

'Cervantes', in *The New Catholic Encyclopedia, s.v.*

Caso González, José, 'La génesis del *Lazarillo de Tormes*', *Archivum*, 16 (1966), 129–55

ed., *La vida de Lazarillo de Tormes y de sus fortunas y adversidades* (Madrid, 1967)

Cassirer, Ernst, *Das Erkenntnisproblem in der Philosophie und Wissenschaft der neueren Zeit* (Berlin, 1906)

Castellet, José M., *La hora del lector* (Barcelona, 1957)

Castro, Américo, *Hacia Cervantes*, second edition (Madrid, 1960)

Cervantes y los casticismos españoles (Madrid, 1966)

Cavillac, Michel, ed., Cristóbal Pérez de Herrera, *Discursos del amparo de los legítimos pobres* (Madrid, 1975)

'Mateo Alemán et la modernité', *Bulletin hispanique*, 82 (1980), 380–401

and Cecile Cavillac, 'À propos du *Buscón* et du *Guzmán de Alfarache*', *Bulletin hispanique*, 75 (1973), 114–31

Cesarini Martinelli, L., ed., A. Poliziano, *Commento inedito alle 'Selve' di Stazio* (Florence, 1978)

Chapman, K. P., '*Lazarillo de Tormes*, a jest-book, and Benedik', *Modern Language Review*, 55 (1960), 565–7

Chevalier, Maxime, *Lectura y lectores en la España del siglo XVI y XVII* (Madrid, 1976)

'De los cuentos tradicionales a la picaresca', in *La picaresca* (Madrid, 1979), pp. 335–45

'Des contes au roman: l'éducation de Lazarille', *Bulletin hispanique*, 81 (1979), 189–99

Ciplijauskaité, Biruté, ed., Luis de Góngora, *Sonetos completos* (Madrid, 1969)

Clotas, Salvador, 'Meditación precipitada y no premeditada sobre la novela en lengua castellana', *Cuadernos para el Diálogo*, 14 (May 1969); reprinted in Salvador Clotas and Pere Grimferrer, *30 años de literatura en España* (Barcelona, 1971)

Colie, R. L., *Paradoxia Epidemica. The Renaissance Tradition of Paradox* (Princeton, 1966)

Colomer, Eusebio, 'Individuo e cosmo in Nicolò Cusano e Giovanni Pico', in *L'opera e il pensiero di Pico della Mirandola* (Florence, 1965), pp. 53–102

Cortazar, Celina Sabor de, 'Notas para el estudio de la estructura del *Guzmán de Alfarache*', *Filología*, 8 (1962), 79–95

Cossío, José M. de, ed., Fray Antonio de Guevara, *Epístolas familiares* (Madrid, 1950)
    ed., *Autobiografías de soldados (siglo XVII)* (Madrid, 1956)

Courcelle, P., *'Connais-toi toi-même' de Socrate à Saint Bernard* (Paris, 1974–5)

Cros, Edmond, *Protée et le gueux. Recherches sur les origines et la nature du récit picaresque dans 'Guzmán de Alfarache'* (Paris, 1967)
    Contribution à l'étude des sources de 'Guzmán de Alfarache' (Montpellier, 1967)
    Ideología y genética textual. El caso del 'Buscón' (Madrid, 1980)

Dalai Emiliani, M., ed., *La prospettiva rinascimentale: codificazioni e trasgressioni* (Florence, 1979–80)

Démoris, R., *Le roman à la première personne, du classicisme aux Lumières* (Paris, 1975)

Deyermond, A. D., *'Lazarillo de Tormes'. A Critical Guide* (London, 1975)

Díaz-Migoyo, Gonzalo, 'Las fechas en y de El Buscón de Quevedo', *Hispanic Review*, 48 (1980), 171–93
    Estructura de la novela. Anatomía de 'El Buscón' (Madrid, 1978)

Dunn, P. N., *Castillo Solórzano and the Decline of the Spanish Novel* (Oxford, 1952)
    'Problems of a model for the picaresque and the case of Quevedo's *Buscón*', *Bulletin of Hispanic Studies*, 59 (1982), 95–105

Durand, Frank, 'The author and Lázaro: levels of comic meaning', *Bulletin of Hispanic Studies*, 45 (1968), 89–101

Eco, Umberto, *Apocalittici e integrati*, third edition (Milan, 1974)

Egido, Aurora, 'Retablo carnavalesco del buscón don Pablos', *Hispanic Review*, 46 (1978), 173–97

Ernout, A., and F. Thomas, *Syntaxe latine*, second edition (Paris, 1959)

Faral, Edmond, *Les arts poétiques du XIIe et du XIIIe siècle* (Paris, 1958)

Foulché-Delbosc, R., ed., ' "La vida del ganapán" ', *Revue hispanique*, 9 (1902), 291–2

Frenk, Margit, 'Tiempo y narrador en el *Lazarillo* (Episodio del ciego)', *Nueva revista de filología hispánica*, 24 (1975), 197–218

García Berrio, Antonio, *Introducción a la poética clasicista: Cascales* (Barcelona, 1975)

Formación de la teoría literaria moderna (Madrid/Murcia, 1977–80)

García de la Concha, Víctor, 'La intención religiosa del *Lazarillo*', *Revista de filología española*, 55 (1972), 243–77

Nueva lectura del 'Lazarillo' (Madrid, 1981)

García Morales, Justo, ed., Fray Pedro Malón de Chaide, *Libro de la conversión de la Magdalena* (Madrid, n.d.)

García Pelayo, Manuel, *El reino de Dios, arquetipo político* (Madrid, 1959)

Gargano, Antonio, ed., Francisco de Quevedo, *Vida del Buscón, llamado don Pablos* (Barcelona, 1982)

Garin, Eugenio, ed., *Prosatori latini del Quattrocento* (Milan/Naples, 1952)

L'umanesimo italiano (Bari, 1965)

Genéreux Carrasco, H., ed., Licenciado Gregorio González, *El Guitón Honofre* (Valencia, 1973)

Gili Gaya, Samuel, *Tesoro lexicográfico*, vol. I, (Madrid, 1960)

Gillet, Joseph E., *Propalladia and Other Works of Bartolomé de Torres Naharro*, vols. I–III (Bryn Mawr, Pennsylvania, 1943–1951); vol. IV: *Torres Naharro and the Drama of the Renaissance*, ed. Otis H. Green (Philadelphia, 1961)

Gilman, Stephen, 'The death of Lazarillo de Tormes', *PMLA*, 81 (1966), 149–66

González de Amezúa, Agustín, *Cervantes, creador de la novela corta española* (Madrid, 1958)

Goytisolo, Juan, 'Estebanillo González, hombre de buen humor', in his book *El furgón de cola* (Paris, 1967, and Barcelona, 1976)

Green, O. H., 'Sobre las dos fortunas', in *Studia philologica. Homenaje ofrecido a Dámaso Alonso*, vol. II (Madrid, 1960), pp. 143–54

Spain and the Western Tradition, vol. III (Madison and Milwaukee, 1965)

Guillén, Claudio, 'La disposición temporal del *Lazarillo de Tormes*', *Hispanic Review*, 25 (1957), 264–79

'Toward a definition of the picaresque', in *Actes du IIIe congrès de l'Association Internationale de Littérature Comparée* (The Hague, 1962), pp. 252–66; reprinted in his book *Literature as System* (Princeton, 1971), pp. 71–106

ed., *'Lazarillo de Tormes' and 'El Abencerraje'* (New York, 1966)

'Luis Sánchez, Ginés de Pasamonte y los inventores del género picaresco', in *Homenaje a Rodríguez-Moñino* (Madrid, 1966), vol. I, pp. 226–31

Haan, F. de, 'Pícaros y ganapanes', in *Homenaje a Menéndez Pelayo*, vol. II (Madrid, 1899), pp. 149–90

Haley, G., *Vicente Espinel and Marcos de Obregón. A Life and Its Literary Representation* (Providence, Rhode Island, 1959)

Hanrahan, T., SJ, *La mujer en la novela picaresca de Mateo Alemán* (Madrid, 1964)

Herrero García, Miguel, *Madrid en el teatro* (Madrid, 1963)

Ife, B. W., ed., Francisco de Quevedo, *Vida del Buscón, llamado don Pablos* (Oxford, 1977)

Jammes, Robert, *Études sur l'oeuvre poétique de Góngora* (Bordeaux, 1967)

Johnson, Carrol B., *Inside Guzmán de Alfarache* (Berkeley/Los Angeles, 1978)

'Mateo Alemán y sus fuentes literarias', *Nueva revista de filología hispánica*, 38 (1979), 360–74

Joly, Monique, *La bourle et son interprétation. Recherches sur le passage de la facétie au roman (Espagne XVIe–XVIIe siècles)* (unpublished doctoral thesis; in press)

Jones, W. K., 'Estebanillo González', *Revue hispanique*, 77 (1929), 201–45

Juliá Martínez, Eduardo, ed., Juan de Timoneda, *Obras* (Madrid, 1948)

Kaiser, W., *Praisers of Folly: Erasmus, Rabelais, Shakespeare* (Cambridge, Mass., 1963)

Kristeller, Paul Oskar, *Renaissance Thought* (New York, 1965)
Eight Philosophers of the Italian Renaissance (Stanford, 1966)
Renaissance Thought and Its Sources (New York, 1979)

Lanser, S. S., *The Narrative Act. Point of View in Prose Fiction* (Princeton, NJ, 1981)

Lapesa, Rafael, 'Un ejemplo de prosa retórica a fines del siglo xiv: los *Soliloquios* de fray Pedro Fernández Pecha', in *Poetas y prosistas de ayer y de hoy* (Madrid, 1977), pp. 9–24

Laurenti, J. L., *Vida de Lazarillo de Tormes. Estudio crítico de la Segunda Parte de Juan de Luna* (Mexico, 1965)
ed., Juan de Luna, *Segunda Parte de la Vida de Lazarillo de Tormes* (Madrid, 1979)

Lázaro Carreter, Fernando, 'Originalidad del *Buscón*', in *Studia philologica. Homenaje a Dámaso Alonso*, vol. ii (Madrid, 1960), pp. 319–38
ed., Francisco de Quevedo, *La vida del Buscón, llamado don Pablos* (Salamanca, 1965)
'La ficción autobiográfica en el *Lazarillo de Tormes*', in *Litterae hispanae et lusitanae* (Munich, 1966), pp. 195–213; reprinted in his book *'Lazarillo de Tormes' en la picaresca*, pp. 11–57
'Para una revisión del concepto "novela picaresca" ' (a paper read at the Third International Congress of Hispanists, on 30 August 1968), now in *'Lazarillo de Tormes' en la picaresca*, pp. 193–229
'Construcción y sentido del *Lazarillo de Tormes*', *Ábaco*, 1 (Madrid,

1969), 45–134; reprinted in *'Lazarillo de Tormes' en la picaresca*, pp. 59–192

'Lazarillo de Tormes' en la picaresca, (Barcelona, 1972)

'Glosas críticas a *Los pícaros en la literatura* de Alexander A. Parker', *Hispanic Review*, 41 (1973), 469–97

'Quevedo: la invención por la palabra', in *Academia literaria renacentista*, vol. II: *Homenaje a Quevedo* (Salamanca, 1982), pp. 8–24

Leclerq, Jacques, *L'amour des lettres et le désir de Dieu. Initiation aux auteurs monastiques du Moyen Age* (Paris, 1957)

Lecoq, A. M., '*Finxit*. Le peintre comme *fictor* au XVIe siècle', *Bibliothèque d'Humanisme et Renaissance*, 37 (1975), 225–43

Levin, Harry, *The Gates of Horn* (New York, 1963)

Lida, Raimundo, 'Pablos de Segovia y su agudeza', in *Homenaje a Casalduero* (Madrid, 1972), pp. 285–98; now reprinted in his book *Prosas de Quevedo* (Barcelona, 1980), together with other related articles, pp. 241–304

Lida de Malkiel, María Rosa, *La originalidad artística de 'La Celestina'* (Buenos Aires, 1962)

'Función del cuento popular en el *Lazarillo de Tormes*', in *Actas del primer congreso internacional de hispanistas* (Oxford, 1964), pp. 349–59; reprinted in her book *El cuento popular y otros ensayos* (Buenos Aires, 1976), pp. 107–22

'Nuevas notas para la interpretación del *Libro de buen amor*', in *Estudios de literatura española y comparada* (Buenos Aires, 1966), pp. 14–91

'El ambiente concreto en *La Celestina*', in *Estudios dedicados a J. H. Herriott* (Madison, Wisconsin, 1966), pp. 145–64

Mainer, José Carlos, 'Notas a una nueva edición de la picaresca', *Insula*, 266 (January, 1969)

Maldonado, F. R. C, ed., E. de Salazar, *Cartas* (Madrid, 1966)

Malkiel, Yakov, 'El núcleo del problema etimológico de *pícaro-picardía*. En torno al proceso de préstamo doble', in *Studia hispanica in honorem R. Lapesa*, vol. II (Madrid, 1974), pp. 307–42

Mancing, H., 'The deceptiveness of *Lazarillo de Tormes*', *PMLA*, 90 (1975), 426–32

Marasso, Arturo, *Estudios de literatura castellana* (Buenos Aires, 1955)

Maravall, José Antonio, *Carlos V y el pensamiento político del Renacimiento* (Madrid, 1960)

El mundo social de 'La Celestina' (Madrid, 1964)

'La aspiración social de "medro" en la novela picaresca', *Cuadernos hispanoamericanos*, 312 (June, 1976), 590–625

'Relaciones de dependencia e integración social: criados, graciosos y pícaros', *Ideologies and Literature*, I, no. 4 (1977), 3–32

Poder, honor y élites en el siglo XVII (Madrid, 1979)

Marichal, J., *La voluntad de estilo* (Barcelona, 1957)

Maristany, Luis, 'La concepción barojiana de la figura del golfo', *Bulletin of Hispanic Studies*, 45 (1968), 102–22

Márquez Villanueva, Francisco, 'La actitud espiritual del *Lazarillo de Tormes*', in *Espiritualidad y literatura en el siglo XVI* (Madrid, 1968), pp. 67–137

Mäurer-Rothenberger, F., *Die Mitteilungen des 'Guzmán de Alfarache'* (Berlin, 1967)

McGrady, Donald, *Mateo Alemán* (New York, 1968)
'Social irony in *Lazarillo de Tormes* and its implications for authorship', *Romance Philology*, 23 (1969–70), 557–67

Meregalli, Franco, 'La existencia de Estebanillo González', *Revista de literatura*, 41 (1979), 55–67

Meseguer Fernández, J., ed., Fray Juan de Pineda, *Diálogos familiares de la agricultura cristiana* (Madrid, 1963)

Millé y Jiménez, J., ed., *Estebanillo González* (Madrid, 1934)

Miller, Stuart, *The Picaresque Novel* (Cleveland, 1967)

Molho, Maurice, prologue to *Romans picaresques espagnols* (Paris, 1968); published independently in Spanish as *Introducción al pensamiento picaresco* (Salamanca, 1972)
'Cinco lecciones sobre el *Buscón*', in his book *Semántica y poética (Góngora, Quevedo)* (Barcelona, 1977), pp. 89–131

Monte, A. del, *Itinerario del romanzo picaresco spagnolo* (Florence, 1957)

Moore, E.R., 'Estebanillo González's travels in southern Europe', *Hispanic Review*, 8 (1940), 24–45

Moreno Báez, Enrique, *Lección y sentido del 'Guzmán de Alfarache'* (Madrid, 1948)
Nosotros y nuestros clásicos, second edition (Madrid, 1968)

Morreale, Margherita, *Pedro Simón Abril* (Madrid, 1949)

Morris, C. B., *The Unity and Structure of Quevedo's 'Buscón': 'Desgracias encadenadas'* (Hull, 1965)

Muñoz Delgado, Vicente, *Lógica, ciencia y humanismo en la renovación teológica de Vitoria y Cano* (Madrid, 1980)

Mylne, V. G., *The Eighteenth-Century French Novel. Techniques of Illusion*, second edition (Cambridge, 1981)

Nelson, W., *Fact or Fiction. The Dilemma of the Renaissance Storyteller* (Cambridge, Mass., 1973)

Nerlich, M., 'Plädoyer für Lázaro: Bemerkungen zu einer Gattung', *Romanische Forschungen*, 80 (1968), 354–94

Ortega y Gasset, José, *El tema de nuestro tiempo*, in his *Obras completas*, second edition, vol. III (Madrid, 1950)

Pacheco, Arsenio, ed., Gonzalo de Céspedes y Meneses, *Varia fortuna del soldado Píndaro* (Madrid, 1975)

Pamp de Avalle-Arce, Diane, ed., Francesillo de Zúñiga, *Crónica burlesca del emperador Carlos V* (Barcelona, 1981)

Panofsky, E., 'Albrecht Dürer and classical antiquity', in *Meaning in the Visual Arts* (Garden City, NY, 1955), pp. 236–94

Renaissance and Renascenses in Western Art (Copenhagen, 1960)

Parker, A. A., *Literature and the Delinquent. The Picaresque Novel in Spain and Europe, 1599–1753* (Edinburgh, 1967); Spanish enlarged translation: *Los pícaros en la literatura* (Madrid, 1971)

Peale, C. George, '*Guzmán de Alfarache* como discurso oral', *Journal of Hispanic Philology*, 4 (1979), 25–57

Pérez, Joseph, 'La unidad religiosa en la España del siglo XVI', in *Seis lecciones sobre la España de los Siglos de Oro. Homenaje a M. Bataillon* (Seville/Bordeaux, 1981), pp. 95–110

Potts, L. J., *Aristotle on the Art of Fiction* (Cambridge, 1968)

Pring-Mill, R. D. F., 'Some techniques of representation in the *Sueños* and the *Criticón*', *Bulletin of Hispanic Studies*, 45 (1968), 270–84

Puyol y Alonso, J., ed., Francisco López de Úbeda, *Libro de entretenimiento de la pícara Justina* (Madrid, 1912)

Redondo, Agustín, 'Del personaje de don Diego Coronel a una nueva interpretación de *El Buscón*', in *Actas del quinto congreso internacional de hispanistas* (Bordeaux, 1977), pp. 699–711

'Historia y literatura: el personaje del escudero de *El Lazarillo*', in *La picaresca* (Madrid, 1979), pp. 421–35

Révah, I. S., 'Un pamphlet contre l'Inquisition d'Antonio Enríquez Gómez: la seconde partie de la *Política Angélica*', *Revue des études juives*, 131 (1962), 81–168

Rey, Alfonso, 'La novela picaresca y el narrador fidedigno', *Hispanic Review*, 47 (1979), 55–75

Rey Hazas, A., ed., Francisco López de Úbeda, *Libro de entretenimiento de la pícara Justina* (Madrid, 1977)

Ricard, Robert, *Estudios de literatura religiosa española* (Madrid, 1964)

Rico, Francisco, 'Problemas del *Lazarillo*', *Boletín de la Real Academia Española*, 46 (1966), 277–96

ed., *La novela picaresca española*, vol. I (Barcelona, 1967 [1966])

'Sobre el origen de la autobiografía en el *Libro de buen amor*', *Anuario de estudios medievales*, 4 (1967), 301–25

'Estructuras y reflejos de estructuras en el *Guzmán de Alfarache*', *Modern Language Notes*, 82 (1967), 171–84

'*El Caballero de Olmedo*: amor, muerte, ironía', *Papeles de Son Armadans*, no. 139 (October, 1967); a revised version can be found in F. Rico, ed., Lope de Vega, *El Caballero de Olmedo*, third edition (Madrid, 1981)

El pequeño mundo del hombre. Varia fortuna de una idea en las letras españolas (Madrid, 1970)

'En torno al texto crítico del *Lazarillo de Tormes*', *Hispanic Review*, 38 (1970), 405–19

Vida u obra de Petrarca, vol. I: *Lectura del 'Secretum'* (Padua/Chapel Hill, 1974)

'Para el prólogo del *Lazarillo*: "el deseo de alabanza" ', in *Actes de la Table Ronde . . . Picaresque Espagnole* (Montpellier, 1976), pp. 101–16

'*Laudes litterarum*: humanisme et dignité de l'homme dans l'Espagne de la Renaissance', in Agustín Redondo, ed., *L'humanisme dans les lettres espagnoles* (Paris, 1979), pp. 31–50

ed., *Lazarillo de Tormes* (Barcelona, 1980)

Primera cuarentena (Barcelona, 1982)

'Nuevos apuntes sobre la carta de Lázaro de Tormes', in *Homenaje a Fernando Lázaro Carreter* (Madrid, 1983)

ed., M. Alemán, *Guzmán de Alfarache* (Barcelona, 1983)

Riley, E. C., *Cervantes's Theory of the Novel* (Oxford, 1962)

Ríos, Blanca de los, ed., Tirso de Molina, *Obras*, vol. I (Madrid, 1946)

Riquer, Martín de, ed., S. de Covarrubias, *Tesoro de la lengua castellana* (Barcelona, 1943)

ed., *La Celestina y Lazarillos* (Barcelona, 1959)

ed., Miguel de Cervantes, *Don Quijote* (Barcelona, 1962)

Rivers, Elias L., 'Para la sintaxis del soneto', in *Studia Philologica. Homenaje ofrecido a Dámaso Alonso*, vol. III (Madrid, 1963), pp. 225–33

Robbe-Grillet, Alain, *Pour un nouveau roman* (Paris, 1963)

Rodríguez Marín, Francisco, ed., C. Suárez de Figueroa, *El pasajero* (Madrid, 1913)

Rojas Garcidueñas, J., ed., Mateo Alemán, *Ortografía castellana*, with a prologue by T. Navarro (Mexico, 1950)

Romberg, B., *Studies in the Narrative Technique of the First-Person Novel* (Stockholm, 1962)

Rouanet, L., ed., *Colección de autos, farsas y coloquios del siglo XVI* (Barcelona/Madrid, 1901)

Rudder, R. S., 'Nueva luz sobre Juan de Luna', in *La picaresca* (Madrid, 1979), pp. 485–91

Rumeau, A., 'Notes au *Lazarillo*: lanzar', *Bulletin hispanique*, 64 (1962), 233–5

'Notes au *Lazarillo*: les éditions d'Anvers. . .', *Bulletin hispanique*, 66 (1964), 257–93

Le 'Lazarillo de Tormes'. Essai d'interprétation, essai d'attribution (Paris, 1964)

Salomon, Noël, 'Algunos problemas de sociología de las literaturas de lengua española', in J.-F. Botrel and S. Salaün, eds., *Creación y público en la literatura española* (Madrid, 1974), pp. 15–39

San Miguel, A., '*Tercera parte del Guzmán de Alfarache*. La promesa de Alemán y su cumplimiento por el portugués Machado de Silva', *Iberoromania*, 1 (1974), 95–120

Sansone, G. E., ed., Juan Cortés de Tolosa, *Lazarillo de Manzanares con otras cinco novelas* (Madrid, 1974)

Schevill, R. and A. Bonilla, eds., M. de Cervantes, *Comedias y entremeses*, vol. III (Madrid, 1918)

M. de Cervantes *Novelas ejemplares*, vol. II (Madrid, 1923)

Scudieri Ruggieri, J., '*Picacantones e pícaros de corte*: contributo alla storia del mondo picaresco', in *Studi di letteratura spagnola* (Rome, 1965), pp. 211–23

Segre, Cesare, 'Punto di vista e plurivocità nell'analisi narratologica', in *Atti del convegno internazionale 'Letterature classiche e narratologia'* (Perugia, 1981), pp. 51–65

Senabre, Ricardo, 'El doctor Carlos García y la picaresca', *Cuadernos para la investigación de la literatura hispánica*, I (1978), 43–54

Shipley, G. A., 'The critic as witness for the prosecution: making the case against Lázaro de Tormes', *PMLA*, 97 (1982), 179–94

Sieber, Harry, 'Apostrophes in the *Buscón*: an approach to Quevedo's narrative technique', *Modern Language Notes*, 83 (1968), 178–211

Language and Society in 'La vida de Lazarillo de Tormes' (Baltimore, 1978)

Sobejano, Gonzalo, 'De la intención y valor del *Guzmán de Alfarache*', *Romanische Forschungen*, 71 (1959), 266–86; reprinted in his *Forma literaria y sensibilidad social* (Madrid, 1967)

'Un perfil de la picaresca: el pícaro hablador', in *Studia hispanica in honorem R. Lapesa*, vol. II (Madrid, 1975), pp. 467–85

'El *Coloquio de los perros* en la picaresca y otros apuntes', *Hispanic Review*, 43 (1975), 25–41

'De Alemán a Cervantes: monólogo y diálogo', in *Homenaje al prof. Muñoz Cortés* (Murcia, 1977), pp. 713–29

'La digresión en la prosa narrativa de Lope de Vega y en su poesía epistolar', in *Estudios ofrecidos a E. Alarcos Llorach*, vol. II (Oviedo, 1978), pp. 469–94

Spitzer, Leo, 'Zur Kunst Quevedos in seinem *Buscón*', in *Romanische Stil-und Literaturstudien*, vol. II (Marburg, 1931); now available in Spanish in G. Sobejano, ed., *Francisco de Quevedo* (Madrid, 1978), pp. 123–84

Lingüística e historia literaria (Madrid, 1955)

Tierno Galván, Enrique, *Sobre la novela picaresca y otros escritos* (Madrid, 1974)

Todorov, T., ed., *Théorie de la littérature. Textes des formalistes russes* (Paris, 1965)

Truman, R. W., 'Parody and irony in the self-portrayal of Lázaro de Tormes', *Modern Language Review*, 63 (1968), 600–5

'Lázaro de Tormes and the *homo novus* tradition', *Modern Language Review*, 64 (1969), 62–7

'*Lazarillo de Tormes*, Petrarch's *De remediis adversae fortunae*, and Erasmus's *Praise of Folly*', *Bulletin of Hispanic Studies*, 52 (1975), 33–53

Varela, José Luis, 'Sobre el realismo cervantino en *Rinconete*', *Atlántida*, 6, no. 35 (1968); reprinted in his book *La transfiguración literaria* (Madrid, 1970)

Vilanova, Antonio, ed., Francisco Delicado, *La lozana andaluza* (Barcelona, 1952)

'L'*Ane d'Or* d'Apulée, source et modèle du *Lazarillo de Tormes*', in Agustín Redondo, ed., *L'humanisme dans les lettres espagnoles* (Paris, 1979), pp. 267–85

Wardropper, Bruce W., 'El trastorno de la moral en el *Lazarillo*', *Nueva revista de filología hispánica*, 15 (1961), 441–7

Watt, Ian, *The Rise of the Novel* (Berkeley, 1962)

Weber de Kurlat, Frida, *Lo cómico en el teatro de Fernan González de Eslava* (Buenos Aires, 1963)

Wenzel, S., *The Sin of Sloth: Acedia in Medieval Thought and Literature* (Chapel Hill, 1967)

Williams, I., *The Idea of the Novel in Europe, 1600–1800* (New York, 1979)

Williamson, E., 'The conflict between author and protagonist in Quevedo's *Buscón*', *Journal of Hispanic Philology*, 2 (1977), 45–59

Wilson, E. M., ed., Fray I. de Buendía, *Triunfo de llaneza* (Madrid, 1970)

Woods, M. J., 'Pitfalls for the moralizer in *Lazarillo de Tormes*', *Modern Language Review*, 74 (1979), 580–98

Ynduráin, Francisco, 'La novela desde la segunda persona. Análisis estructural', in *Prosa novelesca actual* (Madrid, 1968)

Ynduráin, Domingo, 'Algunas notas sobre el "tractado tercero" del *Lazarillo de Tormes*', in *Studia hispanica in honorem R. Lapesa*, vol. III (Madrid, 1975), pp. 507–17

    ed., Francisco de Quevedo, *Vida del Buscón, llamado don Pablos* (Madrid, 1980)

Index